Aleksander Korzhenkov

Zamenhof
*The Life, Works and Ideas
of the Author of Esperanto*

Aleksander Korzhenkov

. . . . . .

Zamenhof

The Life, Works and Ideas
of the Author of Esperanto

. . . . . .

English translation and notes by Ian M. Richmond
Edited by Humphrey Tonkin

. . . . . .

MONDIAL
in cooperation with
Universal Esperanto Association

Mondial
New York

in cooperation with

Universal Esperanto Association
Rotterdam

Aleksander Korzhenkov:
Zamenhof
The Life, Works and Ideas of the Author of Esperanto

Abridged by the author from
Homarano: La vivo, verkoj kaj ideoj de d-ro L.L. Zamenhof
Kaliningrad: Sezonoj; Kaunas: Litova Esperanto-Asocio, 2009

English translation and notes by Ian M. Richmond
Edited by Humphrey Tonkin

Photos: Archives of the Universal Esperanto Associations

ISBN 978-1-59569-167-5
Library of Congress Control Number: 2010926187

www.mondialbooks.com

Contents

Introduction

Esperanto in the World Today

Today, at the beginning of the twenty-first century, the international language Esperanto is a mature language, spoken and used by hundreds of thousands of people across the world, with its own literature and culture, its own native speakers, its own organizations and promotional activities. But it was not always so. Released to the public for the first time in the late nineteenth century (in 1887, to be precise) Esperanto had its specific origins in the fertile brain of a single individual, L. L. Zamenhof, and in the particular circumstances into which he was born and came of age. It is the story of these origins that Aleksander Korzhenkov's biography sets out to tell. That biography was originally published in Esperanto; the present version, in Ian Richmond's excellent translation, is an abridged version of the original text, prepared for English readers by the author.

Zamenhof, as we discover from Korzhenkov, was a child of his times – buffeted by the social upheavals of Eastern Europe in the late nineteenth century, eager to find solutions to these social ills, but alive to the new possibilities brought by technological change, and new ways of thinking that accompanied this change. Eager to solve the specific problems of his own day, he created a language equally well suited to addressing those of ours.

There is much about today's Esperanto movement – or, to give it a more inclusive and accurate name, today's Esperanto language community – that would surprise its originator; but there are also some similarities that might have gratified him. The language has clearly expanded, and continues to expand, to meet new demands and to adapt to new circumstances. It is used today in ways that Zamenhof could not have imagined; even the language has changed. Most people are unaware that the majority of the lexical elements in the language – the words themselves – were not created by Zamenhof, who built only the bare essentials of the language and left it to develop through its community of users. Like all other languages, Esperanto has grown through use: it may have begun in the mind of Zamenhof, but it has been tested and expanded, proven and adapted, by its speakers themselves. Much of the vocabulary is their work, not Zamenhof's.

We sometimes assume that Esperanto was the product of a library or a study – born out of the work of an isolated scholar. But, as Korzhenkov's biography makes clear, this too is erroneous. Esperanto had its beginnings in the musings and invention of a schoolboy, in the unbounded imaginations of a student. It is a young language, with the zest and exuberance of youth; and it carries with it the urgency of the reformist. Zamenhof was all of nineteen years old when he first presented the language to his friends, and a mere twenty-eight when the language was first published. Esperanto has been identified with young people ever since, as any visitor to an international meeting of young Esperantists can see and experience.

Zamenhof's interest in Esperanto was not primarily linguistic, but ethical, and he did not stop his project for international understanding with the creation of Esperanto, going beyond the language to propose a new religious and ethical rapprochement. Nor were Zamenhof's ideas approved by all the original adepts of the language. The specifics of his circumstances were not necessarily shared by others, who saw Esperanto as first and foremost relevant to *their* needs, *their* priorities. These needs and priorities often did not coincide with the utopian ideals of their founder. But there can be no doubt that, if Esperanto is today available for all purposes, it has survived and flourished thanks to the unrelenting moral conviction of its originator. Zamenhof understood that if a planned language such as Esperanto is to survive and grow, it needs more than a belief in nouns and verbs to sustain it.

Although its origins were specific to a particular time and place, Esperanto's uses today span many fields of human endeavour. Zamenhof dreamed that his language would one day be used for all types of interlingual communication, and that dream has largely come true – not always for the best. He dreamed of peace, for example, but on occasion the language was used to justify conflict. When World War I broke out, the German High Command chose Esperanto as one of the languages in which to present its side of the argument for war – even as the newly-formed Universal Esperanto Association worked to reunite families separated by the hostilities, and even as conscientious objectors learned Esperanto in prisons in Britain and elsewhere. Socialists embraced Esperanto, but chambers of commerce did too, and not always in mutual agreement. Esperanto was denounced by Hitler and Stalin, and numerous speakers of Esperanto lost their lives in Stalin's purges only because they used the language to maintain their connections with the larger world. And all but one of Zamenhof's direct descendants were murdered by the Nazi régime.

After World War II, the United States Army, looking for a language to represent the enemy in military manoeuvres, settled on Esperanto, of all languages, to avoid offending anyone else. Thus, for a brief time, Esperanto became, in army parlance, "the aggressor language." Almost from the beginning, the new rulers of China under Mao Zedong used Esperanto to present the revolutionary point of view on Korea and Vietnam. Esperanto was quite widely used in the countries of Eastern Europe under socialism, often as an ancillary to their efforts to sway international public opinion – but the Esperanto movement of Eastern Europe, by maintaining its contacts with the west in an era when such contacts were constricted, helped steer these countries through a peaceful transition when the Wall fell. If Esperanto sometimes makes good propaganda, it is also a language of resistance.

Zamenhof had ideas on the uses and purpose of Esperanto that would seem strange today. He specifically suggested the language as a solution to *internal* language disputes within individual countries, and in fact devoted relatively little attention to its possible use by governments internationally. Soon after his death, efforts were made to interest the League of Nations in its use and adoption, unsuccessfully. Zamenhof's argument was that the world lacks a common means of linguistic communication and needs one – preferably one that promotes linguistic equality among all, since use of a particular national or ethnic language internationally favours the native speakers of that language.

Today that argument has shifted. For the most part, Esperanto speakers no longer argue that there is no way of communicating across languages (though linguistic incomprehension and misunderstandings continue to plague us); but many maintain that such communication in its present form threatens small languages with extinction and undermines the cultural pluralism that is so necessary in a world that in other respects is becoming homogenized and commercialized. Thus one finds Esperanto speakers espousing the cause of linguistic human rights, of cultural diversity, and of sustainable lifestyles. Zamenhof would surely approve of the high ethical standards of many Esperantists, but might be bewildered by the way in which they manifest themselves – in ways so different from those of the world that he inhabited.

Would the language have come into being if Zamenhof had not felt the pressures he felt, had not been born into the environment of anti-Semitism and rising nationalism that he experienced? Any answer to that question would be mere historical speculation – but one thing is clear: the language that Zamenhof invented has endured into the fundamentally altered world of today and gives every indication of continuing to endure. Origins are important, but they tell us only so much.

In one respect Zamenhof was ahead of his time and ahead of his fellow Esperanto-speakers. He recognized the dangers inherent in religious differences at a time when such differences were seen as less of an issue than they are today. Arguably, he felt the difference of religion more than he felt the difference of language in his fellow human beings. He urged tolerance and understanding, but above all he urged cooperation in the creation of international norms of ethical living that would apply to all human beings. His was a voice crying in the wilderness: precious little attention was given to finding such norms in his own day. But, half a century later, many of his beliefs saw fulfilment in the drafting of the Universal Declaration of Human Rights (1948) and other human rights instruments that issued from it. It is significant that the Universal Esperanto Association, even before the Declaration came into force, wrote respect for human rights into its constitution – and that one young diplomat who helped draft the document, Ralph Harry of Australia, was an active Esperantist. This was just one place where the work of the United Nations and the work of the Esperantists intersected.

Later, UNESCO went on to recognize the achievements of Esperanto in bringing people together around common ideals all across the world. Its resolution of 1954 was reinforced by a similar, indeed broader, resolution thirty years later. In 1959, on the occasion of the centennial of Zamenhof's birth, UNESCO recognized Zamenhof as one of the "great personalities" of humankind. Today, the Universal Esperanto Association enjoys formal cooperative relations with both UNESCO and the United Nations, and its staff and volunteers are active in disseminating news and information to Esperanto speakers about the work of these organizations, and doing what they can to support such efforts. The dream of many Esperantists, that one day Esperanto, as a neutral and easily-learned means of linguistic communication, might play a role in facilitating the operations of such organizations as the United Nations and the European Union by enfranchising those whose languages are seldom heard in their deliberations has not yet come true. But it remains an active part of many Esperantists' agendas. In fact, a key element in the platform of the Universal Esperanto Association is a belief in what the Association calls *linguistic democracy* – the creation of an international environment in which we deal with one another in linguistic equality and in which everyone is on an equal footing. Its socalled Prague Manifesto of 1996 lays out this belief.

Although Article 2 of the Universal Declaration of Human Rights asserts that "everyone is entitled to all the rights and freedoms set forth in this Declaration, without distinction of any kind, such as race, colour, sex, language, religion, political or other opinion, national or social origin, property, birth or other status," we know that all too frequently difference of language is used to bar democratic participation, or to limit human rights. A primary task of the Universal Esperanto Association, indeed of all right-thinking people, is to convince the public at large (and their governments) that to discriminate against someone on linguistic grounds is as reprehensible as such discrimination on grounds of race, or sex, or religion.

It is not only because it enables worldwide communication in a spirit of equality that Esperanto is particularly valuable for young people less weighed down by the prejudices of age and of negative past experience. The language in fact holds great pedagogical promise as a schools subject. Experiments have shown that, as a language easily acquired not only by speakers of European languages but also by others, it constitutes an ideal introduction to foreign language study. It is currently being used in this way in a group of schools in the United Kingdom as part of a program known as Project Springboard. The language also has a place in university curricula: courses in interlinguistics (the study of planned language) and Esperanto studies are offered in numbers of universities across the world.

Perhaps the largest boost for Esperanto has been something wholly unimagined by Zamenhof, and well outside the scope of his ideas – namely the internet. Internet learning probably now accounts for more new speakers of Esperanto than all printed textbooks and local courses put together. Vast quantities of material in or on Esperanto are now available over the internet. Esperanto has always been a language larger than its discernible footprint: books in the language have mostly been distributed outside commercial channels, organizations have kept a relatively low profile as they work to provide their members with the services needed to become active Esperantists, and the rich literary and artistic culture of Esperanto has gone on largely unrecognized by those outside Esperanto itself. Today, this invisible community is becoming increasingly visible. The internet, accessible to Esperantists all across the world, is more and more the preferred means of publication, and the preferred place of learning. Formerly isolated, new learners of the language have easy access to spoken Esperanto, not only through conventional spoken material on the internet but also through internet radio; they can find other learners across the world without difficulty, and they have no need to join an organized Esperanto association to enjoy these privileges. Therefore, what was before mostly a movement of membership organizations has become a diverse and often unpredictable speech community.

Thus it would be fair to say that Esperanto has gone in directions both fervently dreamed of and totally unimagined by its founder, but generally in directions that only serve to underline the importance of his work. The Universal Esperanto Association, which I have the honour to represent at the United Nations, is only the strongest of many Esperanto organizations, international, national, and special-interest. Working out of our headquarters in Rotterdam, in the Netherlands, we collaborate with 69 affiliated national associations across the world – from Argentina to Mongolia, from Benin to Canada, from Iceland to Iran – and enjoy active cooperation with many others. We organize a World Congress of Esperanto annually, recently celebrating the 100th anniversary of the founding of the series at Boulogne-sur-mer (1905). These congresses continue to attract several thousand Esperantists from across the world, but today they are only the largest of literally hundreds of such events, for people of all ages and all walks of life. The Universal Esperanto Association runs a library, operates a bookstore, and is a publisher of Esperanto books. Above all, it is an organization that, while eschewing conventional politics, works for ideals of equality and international understanding, democracy and participation, peace through mutual respect. Zamenhof might have expressed these principles differently, for the times were different; but in essence it is the legacy of this remarkable individual that we seek to perpetuate in our work.

Humphrey Tonkin

Past President of the Universal Esperanto Association
Representative of the Association at the United Nations

EDITOR'S NOTE

To set Aleksander Korzhenkov's biography in context,
we have added to this edition a series of brief updates on
the Esperanto language and movement today and provided
bibliographies on Zamenhof and on Esperanto for those who
wish to read more about the language and its author.

Special thanks to Mark Fettes and Jenya Amis for their
assistance in preparing the text and to Ulrich Becker for
seeing it through the publication process.

H. T.

Zamenhof

......

*The Life, Works and Ideas
of the Author of Esperanto*

1

A Russian Jew

Lazar' Markovitch Zamenhof (later known more widely as Ludovic Lazarus Zamenhof)[1] was born on December 15, 1859, into a Jewish family in what was then the Russian city of Bialystock.

Although Bialystock is now in Poland, the city and the region around it changed hands many times over the centuries, passing mostly back and forth between Poland and Russia. From 1569 to 1795, for example, the city was in the Polish part of the Polish-Lithuanian Commonwealth[2]. Following the breakup of the Commonwealth and its division among the Prussian, Russian and Austro-Hungarian empires, for a short time Bialystock became part of Prussia. Under the 1807 Treaty of Tilsit, however, the Russian empire gained the city and the surrounding region.

By the time the Zamenhof family settled there in the 1850s, Bialystock was the regional centre for the Russian administrative district of Grodna, which was located outside the boundaries of the Polish kingdom in a region ceded to the Russian empire by the 1815 Congress of Vienna. Nevertheless, the Kingdom of Poland and the Russian empire shared a very personal connection, the Russian emperor being also the king of Poland. Bialystock's complex political history helps to explain why there is often some confusion about Zamenhof's true nationality.

In the second half of the nineteenth century the population of Zamenhof's birthplace was 65–75% Jewish with the remainder made up of Polish, Russian, German and Belarusian minorities. The surrounding villages were populated mostly by Belarussians and Poles. At that time, Bialystock was known for its rapidly developing textile industry, from which it got the nickname "Manchester of the North." Ninety percent of Bialystock's manufacturers and merchants were Jewish.

It was to this thriving centre of manufacturing and Judaism that Zamenhof's grandfather moved his family in 1857 from the smaller city of Tykocin, not far from Bialystock. In their new home, the younger son of the Zamenhof family, Mark (Mordecai), met and married Liba Rachel Sofer, the daughter of a prominent Jewish merchant, and moved into number 16 Jatke-Gas, called "Butcher's Shop Street" by the Jewish population. Here, the young couple's first child, Lazar' (later known as Ludovic), the future creator of Esperanto, was born on December 15, 1859, the nineteenth day of Kislevo of the year 5620 in the Jewish calendar.

The house on "Butcher's Shop Street" where Zamenhof was born

Ludovic Zamenhof always identified himself as a Russian Jew, but that designation needs some clarification, because the Russian empire was home to various groups of Jews, including Caucasian, Crimean and Bukharan groups. The Zamenhofs belonged to the group known as Litvak Jews. This particular group of Ashkenazi Jews, originally from the former Litva, which included the present-day Lithuania and large parts of north-east Poland, Belarus and Ukraine, spoke a specific dialect of Yiddish, Litvish Yiddish, and looked to Vilnius as their cultural centre. Besides their dialect and their geographical origin, the Litvak Jews differed spiritually and intellectually from other Jewish groups in Russia. Hasidism,[3] for example, which flourished in Ukraine and southern Poland, was less widespread among the Litvak Jews. On the other hand, the intellectual Haskalah movement, which was inspired by the Enlightenment and had first appeared among German Jews toward the end of the 18th century, had more followers among the Litvaks than among the other groups.

For Zamenhof, his Jewishness was at the very heart of his identity. As he wrote much later, when Esperanto was becoming widely known,

> I am a Jew, and all my ideals, their birth, maturity and steadfastness, the entire history of my constant inner and external conflicts, all are indissolubly linked to my Jewishness. I have never hidden the fact that I am a Jew; every Esperantist knows my ethnicity. I am proud to count myself a member of this ancient people, which has suffered so much and fought so hard, and whose sole mission in history consists, in my opinion, of uniting the peoples of the world under the banner of "one God", that is to say, in a single ideal for the whole of humankind.... If I had not been a Jew from the ghetto, the idea of uniting humanity either would never have entered my head or it would never have gripped me so tenaciously throughout my entire life. No one can feel more strongly than a ghetto Jew the sadness of dissension among peoples.... My Jewishness is the main reason why, from my earliest childhood, I gave myself wholly to one overarching idea and dream, that of bringing together in brotherhood all of humanity. That idea is the vital element and the purpose of my whole life. The Esperanto project is merely a part of that idea; I am constantly thinking and dreaming about the rest of it.
>
> (Letter to Michaux, 1905: *Mi estas Homo* 99,100)

Zamenhof's Jewishness would later be the cause of much unease among leading Esperantists of the early period, who often tried to obscure his ethnicity with the neutral statement that he was a Warsaw physician. Following the first Universal Congress of Esperanto in Boulogne-sur-mer in 1905, for example, the Parisian Esperantist Émile Javal wrote to Zamenhof that of more than seven hundred articles about Esperanto published on the occasion of the Congress only one mentioned his Jewishness. For their part, Polish Esperantists, including "the first historian of Esperanto," Adam Zakrzewski, tried to present Esperanto's creator as a Pole, rather than a Russian, because he lived for many years in Warsaw.

*Location of Bialystock, in Russia,
near the border with Prussia, around 1900 ...*

... and in today's Poland.

Early influences

Zamenhof's mother tongue was Russian, however. He was educated in that language and used it at home and in his family circle throughout his life. As a child, he even dreamt of writing poetry in Russian and, at the age of ten, wrote a five-act classical tragedy in that language. This dual cultural heritage – Russian and Jewish – was shared with his father, Mark. Unlike most Russian Jews of his time, who were trades-people, merchants or doctors,[4] Mark Zamenhof had opted for schol-arly pursuits. After moving to Bialystock, Mark worked as bookkeeper and language instructor to the wealthy Zabłudowski family. Later, he co-founded a school for Jewish girls, in which he taught languages. Among his scholarly pursuits, Mark authored two textbooks while living in Bialystock, *An Introductory Course in General Geography for Elementary Schools* (Warsaw, 1869) and *A Textbook of the German Lan-guage for Russian Young People* (Warsaw, 1871).

In January 1863, little more than three years after Ludovic Zamen-hof's birth, the Polish regions of the Russian Empire erupted as the Poles sought independence from Russian control. Although the Litvak Jews had their origin in the former Litva region, where the rebellion was centred, the majority of them, including the Zamenhofs, did not sup-port the rebels. The rebellion was severely suppressed by the Russian authorities and lasted little more than a year. The Litvak Jews' loyalty to the Russian Empire earned them the good graces of the authorities. Consequently, following the rebellion, Mark Zamenhof was granted a teaching post at a state-run school for Jews and thereby joined the ranks of the Russian civil service, which gave him both a good salary and a stable career. Indeed he was later (1883) appointed to the posi-tion of censor with responsibility for vetting German newspapers, and later also Hebrew and Yiddish publications.

Mark Zamenhof attempted to combine his ethnic-religious and his national identities. Nachum Sokolov, editor of the Warsaw Hebrew-language newspaper *Hacefira* (also spelled *Hazefirah*, "time" or "the dawn") and later secretary general and president of the World Zionism Organization, accurately described Mark's cultural duality when he wrote:

> [He] belonged to two worlds: to the patriarchal, orthodox and traditionalist world through his customary daily life, but also to that of a conscious assimilationist tendency with which he sympathized. This inner conflict between the two cultural tendencies and between the two ways of life made him, the father, a tragic figure... He was highly educated in the area of Judaism – he was a brilliant Hebrew stylist and an erudite Talmudic scholar – yet he adhered to the cultural movement of the "Maskilim" (the Enlightened Ones)[5], who promoted the assimilation of the Jewish populations into the reigning culture, preserving only the religious difference.
>
> (Kohen-Cedek, 199)

Zamenhof's education

The young Zamenhof was thus exposed, through his family, to intellectual and cultural ideas beyond the strict realm of traditional Judaism. His education also took place in the broader world of the reigning culture. In 1870, he began studies in the Bialystock Gymnasium, where he remained a student until late 1873, when his father moved the family to Warsaw to take up a teaching position at the Warsaw Veterinary School and the Real School (a type of Gymnasium).[6] Mark Zamenhof was one of only three Jews teaching in Warsaw's secondary schools at that time; he later went on to teach at the Women's Gymnasium and the First Men's Pro-Gymnasium (a junior school). As the son of a secondary-school teacher, Ludovic received free tuition. In Warsaw, he enrolled in the Second Men's Gymnasium, but was not able to begin his studies immediately. He studied at home for several months in order to learn Latin and Greek, which had not been taught at the Bialystock Gymnasium, but were required for the Warsaw school. He did not return to school until August of 1874.

Ludovic did not spend all his time studying, however. From his earliest childhood, he had reflected on the situation of the Jews, on the relations between peoples and on the possibility of an inter-ethnic language. His father was not at all happy about his son's interest in an international language. Ludovic's brother Lev once wrote that their father "spoke about his son's work to the director of a Warsaw Gymnasium who told him that his son was lost forever, that his work was the surest symptom of the onset of an incurable madness"(*Ludovikologiaj biografietoj* 30). Mark Zamenhof made his son promise not to publish his language project until he had finished his university studies, which he began in August of 1879 in the Faculty of Medicine at the Imperial Moscow University.

At the same time as Ludovic Zamenhof, Anton Chekhov, the future short-story writer and dramatist, was also a medical student at the Moscow University. He and Zamenhof had little or no contact outside

Zamenhof in 1879

of their classes, however, because friendships between Jewish and Christian students were rare at that time.

Despite the fact that Jews comprised only 4% of the population of Russia in the late nineteenth century, they made up 12.2% of Gymnasium students and 8.8% of university students. In particular, many Jews studied medicine and law. It was among these students that Zamenhof found friends.

While at Moscow University, Zamenhof wrote the first analysis of Yiddish grammar, *Provo de gramatiko de novjuda lingvo* (Attempt at a Grammar of the New Jewish Language). Written originally in Russian under the pseudonym L. Gamzefon, this study was unpublished for 100 years. The work was finally translated into Esperanto and published by the *Fondumo Esperanto* (Esperanto Foundation) in a parallel Russian–Esperanto edition in 1982.

On the March 1, 1881, the terrorist organization *Narodnaja Volja* (The People's Will) assassinated Czar Alexander II. The situation in Russia quickly became unstable. In several Ukrainian cities pogroms were perpetrated against the Jews. The ideology of *Narodnaja Volja* backed the pogroms as a form of revolutionary conflict. Although only a few Jews were killed – several dozen of the rioters were killed by the police and army – the pogroms worried the new Jewish intelligentsia, who realized that the integration of Jews into Russian society was a failure.

Because of this unstable situation, Zamenhof returned to Warsaw at the end of his second year of studies and enrolled for his third year at Warsaw University in August 1881. Three years later, he received his medical degree and began searching for a suitable place to set up his practice.

In February 1885, Doctor Zamenhof moved to the town of Wiej-sieje in the Suwałki administrative district (now in north-eastern Poland), where his married sister lived, and began to practice there. After four months, however, he decided that he was ill-suited to general practice. Consequently, the young doctor returned to Warsaw and selected ophthalmology as his specialization. For six months he interned in the ophthalmology department of the Warsaw Jewish hospital. In late 1885, he moved to the district capital, Płock (or Plotzk), and began to practise as an ophthalmologist. It quickly became evident to him, however, that his specialized knowledge was insufficient and, in May 1886, he went to Vienna to begin advanced study at the ophthalmology clinic of the Vienna General Hospital. On completion of his studies there, he returned to Warsaw, where the Zamenhof family had moved to number 40 Muranowska Street. It was at this address that he opened his medical office.

In the meantime, Ludovic had made the acquaintance of Clara Zilbernik, the youngest daughter of Sender Lejbovitch Zilbernik, a soap manufacturer and an upstanding member of the Jewish community. On March 18, 1887, Zamenhof and Clara's engagement was announced. The young couple was married on August 9 in Warsaw and set up house at number 19 Przejazd Street in Warsaw.

Clara's dowry of ten thousand roubles was enough for the young family to live on for several years, during which time Zamenhof was expected to make his medical practice profitable. However, with his father-in-law's consent, Zamenhof invested half the dowry in the publication and promotion of his International Language.

4

The origins of Esperanto

Zamenhof had been busy devising an international language ever since his years as a Gymnasium student. When later asked about the development of Esperanto, he explained the principles on which his language planning was based (Letter to Borovko: *Mi estas Homo* 33-38). He had realized early on that in order to be international a language would have to be neutral, belonging to no nation or ethnic group that might be privileged by its use over others who would have to learn and use it as a foreign language. In this respect, the ideal neutral solution would be an ancient language, but he thought Latin and Greek to be too complex for common use.

Accordingly, he began to reflect on a planned language solution. The creation of a language with a large number of grammatical rules and ponderous dictionaries seemed too huge a task for one man, however. Moreover, it was hardly possible to mould an easy-to-learn grammar from those of the Russian, German, French, Polish, Hebrew, Latin, and Greek languages that he spoke from childhood or had learned later.

In his fifth year as a Gymnasium student, Zamenhof was introduced to English and was surprised to find that its grammar was much simpler than those of Latin and Greek. As a result, he began to exclude from his language project superfluous and little-used forms, irregular verbs and other exceptions. In this way, he quickly arrived at a grammar that contained only the most essential rules and could be outlined in only a few pages.

Having solved the problem of an overly complex grammar, Zamenhof was left with the difficulty of learning a vast vocabulary. Initially, he tried to solve the problem by using a series of logically constructed words along the lines of *a, ab, ac, ad... ba, ca, da... e, eb, ec...be, ce, de... aba, aca, ada..., etc* in which each element had a specific meaning. His attempts to use such forms, inspired by the philosophical languages invented in the 17th century, showed him that, despite their rigid logic, they were difficult to learn and almost impossible to memorize. He therefore abandoned logical classification and turned to the vocabularies of the Romance and Germanic languages, selecting especially words that were recognizable internationally. The difficulty with this solution, however, was that the new language's vocabulary would be just as huge as those of the languages it was taken from, since every word in the national language would require an equivalent in the new language.

His solution was to adopt a system of word formation using affixes. Thanks to this system, it was possible to learn only the basic root-word, to which the addition of invariable suffixes and/or prefixes would create words in the same semantic field without the necessity to learn each one separately. For example, the root-word *vend* (=*related to selling*) allows the formation of words like *vendi (to sell), vendejo (store, shop), vendisto (salesperson, salesman), vendistino (salesperson, saleslady), vendaĵo (item for sale)*, etc.

When he began his last year (the eighth) at the Gymnasium, he distributed his Lingwe Uniwersala, an early version of Esperanto, among his classmates. On the 5th of December 1878 in the Zamenhof family home, he celebrated with several classmates "the canonization of the language." On the festive table lay the grammar and dictionary of the new language along with several translations into the Lingwe Uniwersala. Unfortunately, none of these items has survived. The young men reportedly conversed in the new language and enthusiastically sang the anthem

> *Malamikete de las nacjes*
> *Kadó, kadó, jam temp' está!*
> *La tot' homoze in familje*
> *Konunigare so debá.*

(Hostile barriers between peoples,
Fall, fall, it is time!
The whole of humanity
Must come together as one family.)

Although only the name "Lingwe Uniwersala" and the above four-line anthem have survived from this early project, it is clear that it was based on the same three main principles as present-day Esperanto: an international vocabulary, a regular grammar and word formation using affixes.

A few months later, the devotees of Lingwe Uniwersala graduated from the Gymnasium and went their separate ways. Zamenhof's language project was suspended for a short time while he studied for his final exams and then because of his move to Moscow. Once settled in Moscow, however, he continued work on his project and sometimes made serious changes to the language. Each time he made a significant change, he produced original texts and translations in order to try out all aspects of his language. Of these interim projects, only a few texts have survived. These are contained in three notebooks Zamenhof used for his *Lingvo universala* during the summer vacations of 1881 and 1882.

It is interesting to note that, for today's Esperantists, the language of the notebooks from 1881 and 1882 is more difficult to understand than the anthem from 1878, even though the notebooks are closer in time to the final version of Esperanto. The main reason for this is Zamenhof's use in the notebooks of a great number of one-syllable roots whose origin is barely recognizable. These short words and one-syllable roots for the most frequent words resulted from the influence on Zamenhof's new language of the newly popular international language project, Volapük. However, Volapük's influence on Zamenhof was ephemeral.[7]

He continued working on his language, perfecting it and rejecting whatever might be superfluous to its development. Most importantly, he paid less and less attention to inventing new details, and more and more to making it harmonious, investing the language as a whole with a definable spirit. That was the effect of the five years he spent polishing the language.

5

Esperanto is born

The international language project was put into its final form in the spring of 1885 in Wiejsieje, where Zamenhof had begun to practise medicine. He spent the next two years looking for a publisher until his prospective father-in-law, Sender Zilbernik, even before the marriage, suggested paying for the publication out of his daughter's dowry. The Warsaw printer Chaim Kelter gladly agreed to take on the work. On the 14th of July, 1887, after typesetting and vetting by the censor, the 42-page booklet appeared under the title, *Meždunarodny' jazyk. Predislovije i polnyj učebnik (por Rusoj)*, i.e. *International Language. Foreword and Complete Textbook (For Russian Speakers)*. The 27-year-old author hid himself behind the pseudonym D-ro Esperanto, Doctor Hopeful. This publication date (July 26 in the Gregorian calendar) is considered Esperanto's birthdate.

Before the end of the year, Kelter printed the Polish, French and German versions of the booklet, which later became popularly known as the *Unua Libro* (First Book). The Russian version had to be reprinted only six months after the initial printing. Translations and adaptations followed in various languages: among others, English (1888); Hebrew, Yiddish, Swedish, Lithuanian (1889); Danish, Bulgarian, Italian, Spanish, Czech (1890).

Zamenhof's *Unua Libro* consisted of four parts, of which the longest was not the *Complete Textbook* (*Plena lernolibro*), but rather the *Foreword* (*Antaŭparolo*), which filled pages 3 to 30. In the *Foreword*, Zamenhof first talked about the problems language diversity causes in every sphere of life and emphasized particularly that it provokes dissension among peoples. Like many language-project authors, he believed also that an international language would have great practical benefits for science and commerce, as well as for literature, but he placed particular emphasis on "the enormous usefulness to humanity of an international language that, without intruding into peoples' home life, could be a language of government and social interaction, at least in countries with diverse language groups."

The *Foreword* also contains several texts in the international language: *Our Father, Extract from the Bible, A Letter, In a Dream I Saw a Princess* (translation of a poem by Heine), and two original poems by Zamenhof, *Mia penso* (My Thought) and *Ho, mia kor'* (Oh, My Heart).

Conscious of the fact that no one will bother to learn a language that no one else uses, Zamenhof launched, at the same time as his *Unua Libro*, a campaign to have people promise to learn the international language "if it is shown that ten million people have publicly made the same promise." He announced that the names and addresses of the ten million who had made the promise would be published in a separate book.

In addition to the *Foreword*, between its grey covers the Russian version contained

- eight reply coupons bearing the above declaration that could be cut out, filled in and mailed to the author (pp. 31–34);

- a complete textbook of the international language covering six pages and containing the following elements: the alphabet; rules for the parts of speech and general grammar – eight each for a total of sixteen rules (pp. 35–40); permission to translate the booklet into other languages (p. 41); the address of the author: Dr. L. Zamenhof, on behalf of Dr. Esperanto (p. 42);

- an international language / national language dictionary (the Russian version has 917 root words) on both sides of a large sheet of paper;

- the following declaration in the appropriate national language, which appeared on the second page: "An international language, just like a national language, is public property, and the author hereby renounces forever all personal rights to it."

What does Zamenhof's new language look like?

It uses 22 letters of the Latin alphabet, dropping the letters *q, w, x* and *y* and adding six additional letters: *ĉ* [ch], *ĝ* [dj], *ĥ* [guttural ch, as in "loch"], *ĵ* [zh, as in "measure"], *ŝ* [sh], *ŭ* [w]. Each letter represents only one sound. For example, *c* is always pronounced [ts] and never [k] or [s]. The accent in a word always falls on the next-to-last syllable.

The main parts of speech have specific endings: -*o* for the singular noun, -*a* for the singular adjective, -*i* for the infinitive, -*e* for adverbs derived from a root word. Indicative verbs take the ending -*as* for the present tense, -*is* for the past tense and -*os* for the future tense. The ending -*u* expresses a command or a wish and -*us* expresses the conditional. Nouns take the ending –*n* to indicate a direct object and –*j* (pronounced like *y*) to indicate the plural. The ending -*jn* therefore indicates a plural noun used as a direct object.

The lexicon is based mainly on the international words found in the European languages. Words such as *adreso*, *biblioteko*, *centro*, *ĉokolado*, *demokratio*, etc. do not require any effort to memorize for speakers of many different languages. For the remainder, Zamenhof used words from the Romance and Germanic languages and, to a lesser extent, the Slavic languages.

As mentioned above, the word formation makes maximum use of affixes. For example, from the root word *san* (=*related to health*) one can create new words by adding grammatical endings or other affixes with fixed meanings, such as *sano* (*health*), *sana* (*healthy*), *resanigi* (*to cure, to bring back to health*), *malsana* (*ill, sick*), *malsanulo* (*a patient, a sick person*), *malsanulejo* (*hospital, clinic*), etc. Thanks to this agglutinative principle, a mere three thousand root words can create a vocabulary of more than twenty thousand words.

In the *Unua Libro*, Zamenhof asked that criticisms of his language be sent to him and promised that, after one year, the best proposals he received would be incorporated in a special booklet that would give the language its definitive form.

The *Unua Libro* was sent to linguists, rabbis, editors, and associations in various countries. Zamenhof published advertisements in newspapers, mainly in Russia, but he did not get the ten million promises he sought. Consequently, he was not obliged to publish the names and addresses of the respondents, a massive undertaking that would have required the publication of one hundred books of a thousand pages each with a hundred names and addresses on each page. Nevertheless, he did receive hundreds of letters, both positive and negative, and even some that made a joke of the whole business. He also received coupons expressing the desire to learn the new language independently of the ten million "promises". To respond to these letters and coupons and to provide reading material *in* his language rather than *about* it, he published the *Dua Libro de l' Lingvo Internacia* (Second Book of the International Language) in January 1888.

Meanwhile, The American Philosophical Society (APS) of Philadelphia, founded by Benjamin Franklin in 1743, had elected a committee to study three questions:

- Is an international language necessary?
- Is it possible to create such a language?
- What characteristics should such a language have?

The committee decided that (in Zamenhof's summary):

> it is possible to create an international language; that such a language is necessary; and that it must have the simplest and most natural grammar and the simplest spelling and phonology. Its words must sound pleasant to the ear. Its vocabulary must be created from words more or less recognizable to the most serious civilized cultures. The language's final form must not be the fruit of a single person's labours, but the result of the combined efforts of the whole educated world.
>
> (*D-ro Esperanto* 2)

The APS had invited scientific organizations to attend an international congress at which the definitive form of an international language would be worked out. The Society's secretary, Henry Phillips, received the *Dua Libro* after the invitations had been sent and wrote a favourable report on it.

Having learned of the APS initiative and Phillips' favourable view, Zamenhof published in June of 1888 an *Aldono al la "Dua Libro de l' Lingvo Internacia"* (Supplement to the "Second Book of the International Language"). In this supplement, he outlined the APS initiative and Phillips' position and declared that the entire fate of the international language now rested on the congress and that all devotees of his international language must accept and abide by whatever definitive form the congress might give to the language. He further declared that he was henceforth ceasing his own work on it. Unfortunately, the APS received few registrations and the anticipated congress never took place. Zamenhof was consequently forced to reconsider his decision to withdraw from his language's further development.

Since the speakers of the new language needed more words than were published in the *Unua Libro*, Zamenhof published in early 1889 both Russian–International Language and International Language–German dictionaries. Around this time, the language author's pseudonym was adopted as the name of the language: Esperanto.

The first devotees of Esperanto, now called Esperantists, comprised for the most part scholarly Russian and Polish Jews, Russian followers of Tolstoy, Eastern-European freemasons, and speakers of Volapük who had become disenchanted with their language. The Nuremberg International Language Club, founded in 1885, abandoned Volapük at its general meeting on 18th December, 1888, and converted to Esperanto. Thus, the first Esperanto Club made its appearance.

To create a feeling of community among the first Esperantists and to provide them with reading material, Zamenhof decided to publish a periodical. However, his proposal to publish a weekly paper, *La Internaciulo* (*The Internationalist*), was turned down in September 1888 by the main office for publications in Petersburg.

It was not until 1889 that the number of promises to learn Esperanto reached one thousand, i.e. 0.01% of the magic number of ten million. In the first *Adresaro de la personoj kiuj ellernis la lingvon* (Addresses of People Who Have Learned the Language) published by Zamenhof, there were 919 inhabitants of the Russian Empire. Germany was next, with 30 names. The first thousand names included inhabitants of 266 cities in 12 countries. The greatest numbers were in Petersburg (85), Warsaw (78), Odessa (51), Kiev (33), Moscow (28), Vilnius (26). Only two names were registered for Nuremberg, where nevertheless the first issue of the periodical *La Esperantisto* (The Esperantist) was published on September 1st, 1889.

On December 10, 1954, the General Conference of UNESCO, meeting in Montevideo (Uruguay), adopted the following resolution (IV.4.422-4224) on Esperanto:

The General Conference,

Having discussed the report of the Director-General on the international petition in favour of Esperanto (8C/PRG/3),

- Takes note of the results attained by Esperanto in the field of international intellectual relations and the rapprochement of the peoples of the world ;

- Recognizes that these results correspond with the aims and ideals of Unesco ;

- Takes note that several Member States have announced their readiness to introduce or expand the teaching of Esperanto in their schools and higher educational establishments, and requests these Member States to keep the Director-General informed of the results attained in this field ;

- Authorizes the Director-General to follow current developments in the use of Esperanto in education, science and culture, and, to this end, to co-operate with the Universal Esperanto Association in matters concerning both organizations.

6
Esperanto spreads

La Esperantisto's publisher was the president of the Nuremberg International Language Club (Mondlingva Klubo), Christian Schmidt, and its editor was Dr. Esperanto (Dr. L. L. Zamenhof). The first issue contained eight pages and was printed in newspaper format (35 x 26 cm). It opened with a *Prospectus* in French, German and Esperanto. Each of the remaining texts was printed in parallel German and Esperanto versions. The first part of Zamenhof's essay *Esperanto and Volapük* filled four of the eight pages.

Despite the announcement in the prospectus that the paper would appear on the first of every month, only three issues of *La Esperantisto* were published in 1889, each containing parallel German and Esperanto texts. The following year saw only a further nine issues numbered consecutively to the first three to make a full year's volume. The texts in these nine issues were only in Esperanto with supplementary pages on grammar in German. The paper was a hopeless case financially, since the number of subscribers, mostly from Russia, never exceeded three hundred.

In the third issue's lead article, Zamenhof proposed the creation of a worldwide league that would be "the exclusive and absolute authority in our [language] cause". Even though only two people had publicly expressed their opinion of the proposal – both negative – Zamenhof declared in issue number six, published on March 25, 1890, "The International League of Esperantists exists!"

Beginning with the tenth issue, Zamenhof became *La Esperantisto*'s sole editor, although the paper continued to be published in Nuremberg. Schmidt's role was reduced to that of representing the paper before the government of Bavaria. Meanwhile, opinions about Zamenhof's proposed League of Esperantists continued to arrive and were exclusively negative. Finally, in the last issue of 1890, number twelve, Zamenhof called the League "a stillborn child" and concluded that it did not exist.

The international league was a failure, but Esperantists founded associations in several cities, mostly in Germany, Russia and Sweden. The Petersburg association, *Espero* (Hope) was especially important and Zamenhof devoted considerable space to it in *La Esperantisto*. Indeed, Petersburg provided the greatest number of subscribers to Esperanto's first periodical, a number that reached eighty-seven in 1893.

Subscriptions to the paper stagnated in 1891. In August and September, Zamenhof proposed converting *La Esperantisto* to a limited company and issuing founding member cards, but these proposals aroused little interest. He intended to abandon the publication, but it was saved from financial disaster by the German land surveyor Wilhelm Heinrich Trompeter. Trompeter assumed the cost of publication and also paid Zamenhof a monthly salary of a hundred German marks. This was equivalent to the salary of a semi-skilled worker or a beginning low-level bureaucrat in Russia (fifty roubles). Zamenhof kept his position as editor and Trompeter became the publisher, while Schmidt continued to fulfill his role in Bavaria.

The periodical doubled in size to sixteen pages and, at the same time, became more interesting as the financial burden was lifted from Zamenhof's shoulders. He planned the issues, edited them, corresponded with authors, proofed each text for linguistic correctness, prepared the lists of Esperantists' names and addresses, which were temporarily published in *La Esperantisto*, corresponded with the printer, forwarded subscriptions to Nuremberg, and looked after a multitude of other routine editorial matters.

The most important thing, though, was that he himself wrote most of the texts. The texts of the first issues were almost exclusively Zamenhof's, appearing under his own name, under pseudonyms and anonymously. He wrote the first obituary in Esperanto, which was also Esperanto's first hagiographic text. He was responsible for the first recommendations for the promotion of Esperanto. His translations of Andersen's *The Little Mermaid* and Dickens' *The Battle of Life* appeared in serial form.

The increasingly interesting content brought about a substantial increase in the number of subscribers. In 1892, the paper had 544 subscribers in twelve countries (335 in Russia, 124 in Germany, 56 in Sweden, and 29 in other countries) and in 1893 the subscriber list swelled to 889, a record that *La Esperantisto* never improved upon.

In the meantime, Zamenhof produced several books about the language, including the *Universala Vortaro* (Universal Dictionary), which translated the Esperanto root words into French, English, German, Russian, and Polish.

In April 1892 *La Esperantisto* became simply *Esperantisto* and in January 1893 the subtitle in German and French was dropped from the masthead. In the January issue, Zamenhof again announced the founding of a League of Esperantists. Its membership comprised "all actual Esperantists, i.e. subscribers to our official central periodical". The League's function was to vote on language reforms and organizational proposals put forward by the subscribers. Any subscriber could put forward proposals, but "Each subscriber making a proposal will be required to pay for it at the rate for advertisements." Zamenhof named himself secretary of the League.

Since a number of Esperanto speakers felt that Esperanto was failing to make headway because of inherent linguistic flaws in the language, with the January 1894 issue of *Esperantisto* Zamenhof began publishing a revised language project. His intention was to show what characteristics he would give it if he "were beginning to create the language now, after six and a half years of practical work and trials and hearing so many opinions and so much advice from the widest range of people, newspapers and associations" (3).

The changes were radical. For example, all accented letters and the letter "j" were dropped from the alphabet. Consequently, the alphabet was left with 21 letters, including "h", which Zamenhof said he might well propose dropping in the future. The pronunciation of several letters was changed also: the sound [z] completely disappeared, "c" was to be pronounced [sh] and "z" was to have the sound [ts]. The article was dropped completely. The vocabulary underwent many modifications because of the disappearance of the seven letters and in accordance with the proposal "to avoid German and Slavic words and to use, in so far as possible, only words from the Romance languages."

Once the voting was finished, with 93 in favour of the proposed reforms and 157 opposed, Esperanto remained unchanged. The vote brought stability to Esperanto, but, at the same time, made Esperantists suspicious for a long time of any proposal to found an international organization.

A number of Esperantists, particularly former devotees of Volapük, abandoned Esperanto in the years following the vote. Schmidt, *Esperantisto*'s representative in Bavaria, along with the entire Mondlingva Klubo of Nuremberg, said goodbye to Esperanto and pledged their allegiance to the new language Idiom Neutral.[8] The Nuremberg club's defection meant that there would be no Esperanto club in Germany again before 1903. Even Antoni Grabowski, often called "the father of Esperanto poetry", abandoned Esperanto for almost ten years.

Trompeter, who had wanted the changes, announced that his financial support for the paper would continue only until the year's end. Zamenhof had to take over the running of the paper once again and became the editor/publisher. In 1894, the number of subscribers fell to 596 and this number threatened to fall yet again in 1895 when those who were abandoning Esperanto would fail to renew their subscriptions. In fact the last subscription list shows only 425 paid-up subscribers.

Zamenhof was forced to look for new possibilities. He entered into an agreement with the Tolstoyan editors of the *Posrednik* (Intermediary) publications whereby they would have a continuing column in *Esperantisto*.[9] Perhaps because of this, he won the sympathy of the Tolstoyans for Esperanto, but *Esperantisto* lost its neutrality in the ethical, moral and religious spheres. The column, *Folieto de "Posrednik"* (Posrednik's Leaflet), appeared for the first time in the February 1895 issue. It presented Tolstoy's essay *Prudento aŭ kredo?* (Judgment or Faith?), which caused the Russian censors to forbid the importation of *Esperantisto* into Russia, where it had the majority of its subscribers. Tolstoy himself intervened and had the ban lifted. Nevertheless, after the May-June 1895 issue, which did not appear until August, Zamenhof stopped publishing *Esperantisto*.

(La) Esperantisto played an important role in Esperanto's history. it enabled its readers to become aware of the activities of Esperantists in other countries, to see the regularly updated lists of new Esperantists, to exchange experiences, and to discuss problems with the language. The paper became the seed of the Esperantist "people". Indeed, every subscriber from 1893 on had a vote in the League. In addition, Zamenhof's work on the only Esperanto periodical at that time helped the language, which lacked a basis in tradition, to become stable and unified. The language acquired its own style and orthography and its first abbreviations. The literary texts published in the paper and translated or written by Zamenhof later became the basis of the *Fundamenta Krestomatio* (Basic Anthology).

Following its 1954 resolution, on November 8, 1985, meeting in So-fia, the General Conference of UNESCO again adopted a resolution (11.11) recognizing the progress of Esperanto and celebrating Espe-ranto's centenary:

The General Conference,

Considering that the General Conference at its 1954 session in Montevi-deo, by its resolution IV.1.4.422-4224, took note of the results attained by the international language Esperanto in the field of international intellec-tual exchange and mutual understanding among the peoples of the world, and recognized that those results corresponded with the aims and ideals of Unesco,

Recalling that Esperanto has in the meantime made considerable progress as a means for the advancement of mutual understanding among peoples and cultures of different countries, penetrating most regions of the world and most human activities,

Recognizing the great potential of Esperanto for international understanding and communication among peoples of different nationalities,

Noting the considerable contribution of the Esperanto movement, and espe-cially of the Universal Esperanto Association, to the spreading of information about the activities of Unesco, as well as its participation in those activities,

Aware of the fact that in 1987 Esperanto celebrates its centenary of exist-ence,

1.   Congratulates the Esperanto movement on its centenary ;

2.   Requests the Director-General to continue following with attention the development of Esperanto as a means for better understanding among different nations and cultures ;

3.   Invites the Member States to mark the centenary of Esperanto by suit-able arrangements, declarations, issuing of special postal stamps, etc., and to promote the introduction of a study programme on the language problem and Esperanto in their schools and higher educational institu-tions ;

4.   Recommends that international non-governmental organizations join in celebrating the centenary of Esperanto and consider the possibility of the use of Esperanto as a means for the spreading of all kinds of in-formation among their members, including information on the work of Unesco.

7

A struggling young doctor

Esperanto was having a negative impact on Zamenhof's professional life, however. In the first place, he had to pay for his publications out of his own pocket and therefore needed to earn more money than his fellow doctors, who used their incomes only to support their families. Secondly, Esperanto took a good deal of time that his competitors were able to use for working, professional training and promoting themselves. Finally, not everyone was happy seeing a doctor who was busy creating a language. As a result, his early career was marked by financial difficulties, as he himself wrote:

> Esperanto soon swallowed up the greater part of my wife's money; the rest of it we spent on necessities, for the income from my medical practice was terribly small. At the end of 1889 we were left without a kopeck!
>
> (Letter to Michaux, 1905: *Mi estas Homo* 104)

Ludovic's financial troubles were not the only ones to befall the Zamenhof family at this time. His father, Mark, lost his position as censor at the end of 1888 for having passed a politically suspect text for publication in the Hebrew newspaper *Hacefira* (which was shut down for three months as a result).

In October 1889 Zamenhof prepared the material for the second issue of *La Esperantisto*, sent it to Schmidt, then moved from the Polish Kingdom to Russia to find a city where he could establish a successful practice, preferably without competition. His pregnant wife and his sixteen-month-old son Adam went to Kaunas to stay with Clara's father. Zamenhof tried unsuccessfully to establish himself in Brest (now in Belarus) and in Bialystock, both in the Russian Grodna administrative district. He then went to the district capital of Cherson in southern Ukraine, but a woman oculist was already in practice there. Zamenhof had to compete with her to feed his family, which increased in size on

December 1, 1889, when his daughter Sofia was born in Kaunas. The Cherson experience was a fiasco, so in May 1890 the 30-year-old doctor returned to Warsaw and moved into number 21 Nowolipki Street (his parents still lived in Muranowska Street).

Despite the small salary provided by Trompeter, the family finances were in a bad way. In fact, the family's main support came from the generosity of Clara's father, Sender Zilbernik, for Zamenhof's medical practice was not at all profitable. His gloom deepened when his mother passed away on August 19, 1892. He realized that he could not independently support his family in Warsaw and decided to move to Grodna, where the Jewish population was then in the majority with Russian, Belarussian and Polish minorities also living there.

On October 22, 1893, Zamenhof filled out a form at the medical bureau of the Grodna administrative district requesting permission to set up a medical practice in the city. Having received the necessary permission and finding that the early days of his practice there gave reason to be hopeful, he returned briefly to Warsaw. On November 27th the Zamenhofs, with their two children, left the Polish capital for what would be several years.

In Grodna the family moved into Policejskaja Street in the city centre. Zamenhof's clinic was in the same rented premises. Since his income in Grodna was higher than in Warsaw and the cost of living was lower, Zamenhof intended to remain there for some time. Consequently, he registered himself in the prestigious *Grodna District Yearbook* as a medical practitioner in private practice.

Along with his professional activity and his Esperanto work, Zamenhof still found the time to be active in the Grodna District Medical Society as well as in other areas. As a juror for the Grodna District Court, for example, he took part in trials and distinguished himself by his outstanding integrity and rigour. As an army reserve doctor, he gave notice in writing on June 24th, 1896 that he wished to carry out the duties of a military doctor in Grodna in the event of war.

Working in Grodna in more favourable financial circumstances and a less stressful environment, Zamenhof decided to realize his dream of a Library of the International Language Esperanto (*Biblioteko de la lingvo internacia Esperanto*). The first work to appear in the series was his Esperanto translation of *Hamlet, Prince of Denmark.*

It was a real challenge: to translate the well-known, thought-provoking, heavily nuanced play into a language whose very structure was still under discussion. This was a work of literature "known by everyone", either in the original or in translation, a work studied in every grammar school in the world, brought to the stage by the world's most outstanding actors thousands of times in hundreds of theatres and in dozens of languages. And this unknown eye doctor from the outer regions of Russia accepted the challenge. The first readers were amazed by the translation's fluency, intelligibility and faithfulness to the original. Because of the translation of *Hamlet*, some readers lost all interest in reforming the language, because they became convinced that it was already perfectly functional. One reader even wrote that "reading *Hamlet* in Esperanto was more effective for him ... than all the most expert theoretical arguments" (*Esperantisto* 1895 35-36).

Everything else written or translated by Zamenhof up to the later Hachette period (see the following chapter) and *La Revuo* (The Review) was overshadowed by his translation of *Hamlet*, even the *Ekzercaro* (Collection of Exercises) which received the finishing touches in Grodna and was published in the same *Biblioteko*. Nevertheless, the *Exercises* were a very important publication on account of their many model sentences. They later comprised one of the three constituent parts of the *Fundamento de Esperanto*, the *Foundation of Esperanto*.

The Zamenhofs spent four years in Grodna. After the initial period of prosperity, they again encountered financial problems brought on largely by the appearance in the city of another oculist. In addition, Zilbernik insisted that his grandchildren be educated, not in the small city of Grodna, but in the capital, Warsaw. In the end, Zilbernik made his son-in-law realize that until he had definitively established himself in Warsaw, he must put Esperanto aside and devote himself exclusively to his profession.

Little by little Zamenhof reduced his Esperanto activity, keeping up only the publication of the lists of names and addresses and the most essential correspondence. After the disappearance of *Esperantisto*, he also ceased publishing the *Biblioteko*. For several months, Esperantists had no common link. Finally, in December 1895, *Lingvo Internacia* (International Language) was launched in Sweden. Zamenhof sent it a text from time to time, but played no role in the publication's editorial policy.

His last initiative in Grodna was to plan "a written congress for discussion of and decision on the question of an international language". In early 1897, he prepared a notice about the congress and sent it to six thousand publications and to representatives of various international-language groups, but the poor response it received caused the project to be dropped.

On October 16, 1897, the Zamenhofs left Grodna and returned to live in Warsaw.

UPDATE ON ESPERANTO

Universities and Esperanto:

Many universities include Esperanto in courses on linguistics; a few offer it as a separate subject. Particularly noteworthy is Adam Mickiewicz University, Poznan, Poland, with a certificate program in interlinguistics. The University of California San Diego offers summer courses to learn the language. The North-America-based Esperantic Studies Foundation provides research grants. Scholarly articles, journals, and books on and in Esperanto appear regularly. The Modern Language Association of America's Annual Bibliography records more than 300 scholarly publications on Esperanto every year.

8

The need for an international language

In Warsaw, Zamenhof moved into the house at 19 Dzika Street, located in a poor neighbourhood that had no oculist. He began accepting patients who could not afford to go to his more prestigious colleagues. He also made an effort to obscure the fact that he was the author of a constructed language, so that he would be viewed only as a doctor.

Because his financial circumstances and his social position had been better in Grodna, he, in his own words, "almost went mad from despair". He was forced again to accept money from his father-in-law every month, which he found painful each time. In addition to his reduced financial circumstances and his abandonment of the Esperanto movement, he was nostalgic for Grodna. After four years of living in the province of his birth, Zamenhof did not at first feel at home in Warsaw.

Little by little, however, his income increased and his life settled down. The Zamenhof family's financial situation stabilized in the years 1901–1903, thanks to Zamenhof's daily labours and his preparation of the health certificates required by emigrants, and because of a lucrative contract with the French publishing house Hachette. The family's life became more settled and the couple decided to have another child. A second daughter, Lidia, was born on the 16th of January, 1904.

In the evenings, which he had previously devoted to editing and letter writing, Zamenhof was able to reflect quietly on the problems of the international language and on the fate of the Jews. At the turn of the century, he summed up his thoughts in an essay that he published under a pseudonym. *Essence and Future of the Idea of an International Language* is Zamenhof's longest text about language. It was first published in Esperanto (*Esenco kaj estonteco de la ideo de lingvo internacia*) in the *Basic Anthology of the Esperanto Language* (*Fundamenta Krestomatio de la lingvo Esperanto*) in 1903. According to the note accompanying the title, it is "A report written by Mr. Unuel and read (in a slightly modified and shortened version) by Mr. L. de Beaufront at the congress of the French Association for the Advancement of Science (Paris, 1900)." Because Louis de Beaufront had publicly read the text, many attributed it to him. It was not until 1910, at the Universal Congress of Esperanto in Washington, that Zamenhof admitted in public that he was its author. The pseudonym "Unuel" (Esperanto for "one of") was imitated from the Hebrew pseudonym Achad ha'Am ("One of the people," as in *Genesis* 26:10), used by the Jewish social activist Asher Zvi Hirsch Ginsberg.

The congress of the French Association for the Advancement of Science took place during the Paris World Exhibition in 1900. Many international associations met on that occasion and the language problems at the Paris exhibition served as a spur for introducing Esperanto into their discussions. This was true of associations concerned with modern languages, philosophy, mathematics, comparative history, chambers of commerce, social education, and sociology, among other subjects.

De Beaufront's French-language version of *Essence and Future* appeared in 1901 in the proceedings of the congress. A comparison with Zamenhof's text in the *Fundamenta Krestomatio* reveals that several polemical and promotional passages are missing in the French version. Translations of the Esperanto text were later published in English, Bulgarian, Chinese, French, German, Italian, Japanese, Croatian, Russian, and so on.

In his introduction to the Esperanto version, Zamenhof ranks Esperanto among the ideas which, although very important for humanity, are met initially with distrust and hostility. He compares Esperanto to the discovery of America, the use of steam engines and the introduction of the alphabet. These comparisons show that he thought of Esperanto as a "technical invention."

In logical style, spiced with polemics, Zamenhof deals with the problem in detail, addressing five questions he has posed for himself. According to his logic, everything that is useful and possible, despite the opposition of naysayers, will of necessity be finally accepted if efforts are unrelenting. Thus, people will first come to understand that an international language is useful; then, they will realize that it is attainable; later, they will begin to work on it; and finally, it will gain acceptance either by society itself or by the decision of an international conference. When might this happen? In a year, in ten years, in a hundred years, or even in several hundred years, but sooner or later an international language will win acceptance.

His conclusions were that

1. The adoption of an international language would be hugely useful to humankind.
2. It is entirely possible to introduce the use of an international language.
3. The use of an international language is inevitable sooner or later, however much the naysayers may fight against it.
4. Only an artificial language will ever be chosen as an international language.
5. No language other than Esperanto will ever be chosen as the international language. Either it will be left forever in its present form or changes will be made to it in the future.

In retrospect, Zamenhof's reasoning rested on a few premises widely shared at the time, but now clearly dated. He believed with his whole being that reason and scientific progress would reign in the twentieth century. Yet the twentieth century brought about such triumphs of irrationality as two world wars, genocides, the Holocaust, Hitler, Stalin, Pol Pot, the rise and fall of communist ideology, and widespread disillusionment with the idea of a "bright future" for the majority of Earth's inhabitants.

In Zamenhof's time, seven great powers – Britain, France, Germany, Austria-Hungary, Russia, The United States, and Japan – were rivals and allies of practically equal strength. This meant that the language problem at that time could hardly be solved with one of the languages of the great powers. (Russian and Japanese were less important at that time than English, French and German, which, along with Latin, were considered essential to a good nineteenth-century education.)

The emerging dominance of the United States changed the world order. What has been particularly worrisome for orthodox Esperantists is that the English language quickly met the criteria outlined in Zamenhof's first three conclusions and rendered his fourth and fifth conclusions null and void. Little by little, American English is becoming the primary functioning international language in diplomacy, communications, science, commerce, sport, youth culture, and so on. Modern technology, especially computing, is spread around the world mainly through English.

Esperanto remains a logical and easy-to-learn language, but people learn languages not for their lack of difficulty, but for their usefulness in professional and scientific work, for a more comfortable life, for recreational opportunities, and for cultural and intellectual enrichment. In these respects, Esperanto cannot compete with English. Nevertheless, Esperanto works and its users enjoy not so much the linguistic benefits emphasized by Unuel, as the benefits of a community of Esperanto speakers. Will today's Esperantists succeed in presenting the essence and future of their language in a manner more convincing than Zamenhof's theoretical presentation of more than a hundred years ago?

UPDATE ON ESPERANTO

Libraries:

The Esperanto Association of Britain's library has more than 20,000 items. Other large libraries include the International Esperanto Museum in Vienna (a section of the National Library of Austria), the Hodler Library at the Universal Esperanto Association's headquarters in Rotterdam, and the Esperanto collection in Aalen, Germany. The Vienna and Aalen collections can be consulted through the Internet and international library loan.

9

Esperanto's "French Period"

While Zamenhof remained on the sidelines of the Esperanto movement for five or six years following his return to Warsaw, the French educator Louis de Beaufront, the first successful propagator of Esperanto, was leading it along a new path.

In January 1898, de Beaufront founded the Association for the Advancement of Esperanto (*Societo por la Propagando de Esperanto* or *SPPE*) along with its bilingual periodical *L'Espérantiste* (The Esperantist). He realized that the mystical, fraternalistic ideas of the Slavic and Jewish Esperanto pioneers could not help to advance the language in Western Europe. Dodging the accusation of promoting a double utopia, linguistic and philosophical, he preferred to keep quiet about the reunification of humanity and Esperanto's peace-making role. Instead, he emphasized the linguistic characteristics and the practical usefulness of the international language.

To promote acceptance of the language, de Beaufront sought to recruit influential people. And he succeeded. Among his recruits (and among those recruited by his recruits) were professors and teachers, editors, writers (including Jules Verne), scientists, politicians, jurists, even aristocrats. Their favourable opinions of Esperanto carried more weight in the world than that of a simple eye doctor from Warsaw, because France was still considered to be the world's cultural and intellectual centre.

Among others, the new proselytes included: Émile Boirac, doctor of philosophy and rector of the University of Grenoble (and later of the University of Dijon); Carlo Bourlet, professor of mathematics and prolific author; Théophile Cart, teacher of German at the prestigious Lycée Henri IV and president of the Paris Linguistics Association; General Hippolyte Sebert, member of the Academy of Sciences, a world authority on ballistics, an electronics pioneer, technical director of a powerful steel company, and president of the International Institute of Bibliography.

Bourlet converted the president of the Touring Club de France (TCF), André Ballif, to Esperanto. The 8,000-member TCF supported Esperanto, subsidized groups of Esperantists, started an Esperanto section in its monthly magazine, and made available to Esperantists its facilities outside Paris as well as its Paris headquarters. Cart authored Esperanto textbooks. Boirac publicized in Esperanto university courses for foreigners and began work on a large Esperanto dictionary. Sebert reported on Esperanto to the French Academy of Sciences.

In July 1901 Bourlet arranged a contract between Zamenhof and the famous Paris publishing house *Hachette & Cie*. Hachette began publishing the *Kolekto Aprobita de d-ro Zamenhof* (Collection Approved by Dr. Zamenhof) and paid Zamenhof royalties on each volume in the Collection. Zamenhof also committed himself to publishing his own books only with Hachette. De Beaufront was Zamenhof's representative to Hachette, because the publisher did not want to deal directly with an Eastern European.

De Beaufront's influence soon began to wane, however, because the newly-minted Esperantists – professors, editors, scientists – were more capable organizers and had more social influence than he had. In January 1903, through Bourlet's intervention, Zamenhof's contract with Hachette was revised in a manner advantageous to Zamenhof and Bourlet himself soon took on the role de Beaufront had played.

Following the revision of his contract, Zamenhof again threw himself completely into Esperanto activities. In the same year, he published the *Fundamenta Krestomatio de la Lingvo Esperanto* (Basic Anthology of the Esperanto Language), which he compiled as a model of Esperanto style. It seems that he had planned the anthology while he was still in Grodna in late 1894, because it contains none of the texts from the later *Lingvo Internacia* and *L'Espérantiste*. Indeed, he used only texts from the 1894 Exercises (*Ekzercaro*), from *(La) Esperantisto* (1889–1894, none from 1895), and from Antoni Grabowski's short poetry anthology *La Liro de la Esperantistoj* (The Esperantists' Lyre) of 1893. To these he added a few later texts, including his article *Essence and Future of the Idea of an International Language*.

The Association for the Promotion of Esperanto changed its name in 1903 to French Association for the Promotion of Esperanto (*Societo Franca por Propagando de Esperanto*). The association grew quickly: 1800 members in 1902, 2543 in 1903, 3619 in 1904, and 4052 in 1905. In the latter year, there were 102 functioning local Esperanto groups and 144 Esperanto courses in France.

By June 1905, there were already about thirty Esperanto periodicals. The Esperanto Printing Society (*Presa Esperantista Societo*), the first Esperantist commercial venture in the world, was founded in Paris on February 12 the same year. It was co-owned and co-managed by Cart, who was president, Paul Fruictier, who was commercial director, and Pál Lengyel, the technical director. Fruictier was also the editor of *Lingvo Internacia*, edited by Cart beginning in 1907, and of the *Internacia Scienca Revuo* (International Scientific Journal), published by Hachette.

Esperanto soon spread from France into French-speaking Belgium and Switzerland (the Swiss Esperanto Association was formed in 1903), into the French colonies, and, later, into Italy, Spain and Great Britain.

The Esperanto clubs of Calais and Dover organized the first international meeting, which took place on August 7 and 8, 1904, with two hundred participants, including guests from Algeria, Austria, Belgium, and Germany. During the meeting, the French lawyer Alfred Michaux proposed holding an Esperanto congress a year later in Boulogne-sur-mer, where he was very active in teaching Esperanto.

Esperanto literature:

Esperanto's flourishing literary life has been recognized by PEN International, which includes an Esperanto affiliate. Present-day writers in Esperanto include the novelists Trevor Steele (Australia), István Nemere (Hungary) and Spomenka Štimec (Croatia), poets Baldur Ragnarsson (Iceland), Mikhail Gishpling (Russia / Israel) and Abel Montagut (Catalonia), and essayists and translators Probal Dasgupta (India), Li Shijun (China) and Carlo Minnaja (Italy). Before his recent death, the poet William Auld was twice nominated for the Nobel Prize in Literature. Sutton's *Concise Encyclopedia of the Original Literature of Esperanto* (2008) has entries for over 300 published writers and mentions many more. Literary journals in Esperanto include *Spegulo* (Poland), *Beletra Almanako* (USA) and *Literatura Foiro* (Switzerland).

Music and Esperanto:

Well-established musical genres in Esperanto run the gamut from popular and folk songs through rock music, cabaret, solo and choir pieces, and opera. In addition to these strong grassroots traditions, popular composers and performers in a number of countries have recorded in Esperanto, written scores inspired by the language, or used it in their promotional materials, including Elvis Costello and Michael Jackson. There are several orchestra and chorus pieces that include Esperanto, most notably Lou Harrison's *La Koro-Sutro* and Symphony No. 1 (the "Esperanto"), by David Gaines, both of the USA. Numerous examples of music in Esperanto can be found on-line, including several sites devoted to Esperanto karaoke.

Theatre and cinema:

Plays by dramatists as diverse as Goldoni, Brecht, Shakespeare and Alan Ayckbourn have been performed in recent years in Esperanto. Many plays of Shakespeare exist in Esperanto translation: *Hamlet* was the first to be translated and performed, and more recent Shakespeare performances include a production of *King Lear* in Hanoi, Vietnam. Although Chaplin's *The Great Dictator*, used Esperanto-language signs, feature-length films with dialogue in Esperanto are less common. A notable exception is William Shatner's cult film *Incubus,* whose dialogue is entirely in Esperanto.

10

The first international Esperanto congress

Zamenhof thought the congress in Boulogne-sur-mer would be an opportune occasion for determining the social and linguistic status of Esperanto. He had always wanted to have less responsibility for Esperanto and his yearning for collective responsibility had increased when new leaders appeared in France. In April 1905, he again proposed the creation of a League to resolve the linguistic and organizational problems, but the movement's leaders in France opposed the idea.

Besides the organizational problem, the question of language reform needed to be resolved. Indeed, already the Canadian socialist Albert Saint-Martin had begun using in his periodical *La Lumo* (The Light) an arbitrary alphabet without accented letters. Zamenhof and de Beaufront protested, but the Canadian periodical was supported by the French Jew Émile Javal, who, together with Saint-Martin, encouraged Michaux to put the question of the accented letters on the congress agenda.

As a parliamentarian, Émile Javal was widely known in France because of the "Javal law", which exempted from taxes the parents of seven or more children. He was the director of an ophthalmology clinic, a member of the French Academy of Medicine, the inventor of optical instruments and of an international system for measuring vision (dioptry, 1876). He suffered from poor vision himself for several years and became totally blind in 1900.

Having proved, in his book *Physiology of Reading and Writing* that diacritical marks (accents placed above or below a letter) in the French language caused increased stress on the eyes, Javal could not accept diacritical marks in Esperanto. Because of Javal's expert authority, Zamenhof, the unknown eye doctor from Warsaw, greatly respected his opinion. In fact, Zamenhof and his wife stayed at Javal's home in Paris before the Boulogne congress.

On July 28, after spending several days in Berlin, Zamenhof arrived in Paris for the first time in his life. At the Hachette offices, he discussed a new contract. On the 29th, the Minister of Public Instruction, Jean-Baptiste Bienvenu-Martin, received him and named him a Knight of the Legion of Honour following the decree to that effect signed the same day by French president Émile Loubert and prime minister Maurice Rouvier. At the Esperanto Printing Society he met with Cart, Fruictier and Lengyel. He was received at the Paris City Hall, presided over an awards ceremony for new Esperantists, attended banquets, including one in the Eiffel Tower and a large event in the Hotel Moderne with 250 guests. He also spent a day in Rouen, where he met with Louis de Beaufront.

Prior to Zamenhof's arrival in Paris, Boirac, Bourlet, Cart, Javal, Sebert, and Michaux held a meeting. Michaux read out the Zamenhof's Congress Speech (*Kongresa parolado*) and the poem *Preĝo sub la verda standardo* (Prayer Under the Green Flag)[10] that Zamenhof had sent to him. The others were so shocked by the mysticism of the texts that they decided to persuade Zamenhof at least not to read the *Prayer* at the Boulogne congress.

In Boulogne Zamenhof was invited to a pre-congress dinner with Michaux and the leaders of the Esperanto movement in France, who tried to force him to drop the mystical passages in his speech and not to read the *Prayer*. Zamenhof resisted the pressure. In the end, he agreed to drop only the last verse of the *Prayer*, which expressed a call for the unity of all religions.

The first Universal Congress of Esperanto took place in Boulogne-sur-mer from the 5th to the 13th of August, 1905, and attracted 688 participants from about twenty countries. The fact that Esperanto was the sole working language of the congress generated enthusiasm among the participants and dispelled any fears about the suitability of Esperanto as a spoken language.

The fears of the leading French Esperantists regarding the public's reaction to Zamenhof's opening speech proved groundless. Doctor Esperanto was often interrupted by applause when he spoke of the time when the human family that had been united like brothers with one God in their hearts became strangers to each other because they could no longer communicate, and a state of eternal dissension sprang up among them. Prophets and poets dreamed of a far-off, vague time when human beings would once again begin to understand each other and would again come together as one family. But this was only a dream. He went on to say:

> ... for the first time in human history, we, citizens of the most diverse nations, stand side by side, not as strangers, not as competitors, but as *brothers*, who, understanding each other without forcing our own languages on each other, do not regard each other with suspicion because ignorance divides us, but love each other and shake hands, not in the insincere manner of one foreigner to another, but sincerely, as human to human. Let there be no doubt about the full importance of this day, for today, within the hospitable walls of Boulogne-sur-mer, we are not witnessing a meeting of French with English, Russians with Poles, but of *human beings* with *human beings*. Blessed be this day and may those to come be great and glorious!
>
> (*Mi estas Homo* 108)

This speech by Zamenhof was remembered by the congress participants as one of the most emotional moments of their lives.

The participants were greatly impressed by the theatrical presentation of Molière's *The Forced Marriage*. The congress program included many cultural events, excursions, a Holy Mass in Esperanto, a banquet in the casino, national meetings, working sessions, etc. The working sessions were presided over by Boirac, who navigated smoothly among the interests of competing groups and made sure that the most thorny problems (organizational and linguistic) either received only anodyne solutions or were deferred.

The congress rejected Zamenhof's proposal for a League and for a Central Committee. In this respect, the only decision made was that

The Zamenhof and Michaux families at the first Esperanto Congress, Boulogne 1905

the Congress Executive (president Zamenhof; vice presidents Boirac, Michaux, Sebert, the German Edward Mybs, and the Irishman John Pollen, and four secretaries) would constitute an Organizing Committee for the next congress and would examine the questions that were not successfully resolved at the first congress.

A provisional Language Committee (*Lingva Komitato*) was set up to consult with Zamenhof on questions of language. Its 98 members were named by Zamenhof himself. The question of the accented letters was delegated to the Language Committee, but it took no serious action on it until 1908, when the Committee was reorganized.

The congress's most noteworthy decision was the approval of the Declaration of the Essence of Esperantism, which defined Esperanto both linguistically and socially. Zamenhof's draft of the Boulogne Declaration had contained seven articles, but the Congress Executive edited it down to only five articles.

In the Declaration, Zamenhof avoided pathos and mysticism. It is interesting to note that the first article cites among Esperantism's official goals the role of making peace within multi-ethnic countries, but does not relate Esperanto to peace-making between countries.

The Boulogne Declaration defined the *Fundamento de Esperanto* (Foundation of Esperanto) as the basis of the language. Compiled by Zamenhof before the congress, the *Fundamento* contains a Foreword, the Basic Grammar of 1887, Exercises (1894) and the Universal Dictionary (1893). The Declaration defines an Esperantist as "a person who knows and uses the Esperanto language regardless of its intended use".

At the Boulogne congress, Sebert recommended to the Congress Executive (i.e. the Organizing Committee) that it set up an independent office that would serve as a base for the Language and Organizing Committees, chaired respectively by Boirac and Sebert. Sebert and Javal jointly funded the office.

After the Boulogne congress, Esperanto began to spread quickly, despite the backroom manoeuvres and reformist tendencies of the French leadership. According to the Central Office's statistics, there were 434 Esperanto associations in 1906, 756 in 1907, and 1266 in 1908. A workers' group, *Paco kaj Libereco* (Peace and Freedom), was founded in 1905 and the Esperantist Merchants' Group was formed in 1906, both based in Paris.

Translation into Esperanto:

Recent literary translations include Shakespeare's *The Winter's Tale*, Tolkien's *The Lord of the Rings*, Manzoni's *The Betrothed*, Cabell's *Jurgen*, García Márquez's *One Hundred Years of Solitude*, Umar Khayyam's *Rubaiyat*, Dante's *Purgatorio* (for the third time), Marco Polo's *Book of Wonders*, and Cao Xueqin's great family saga *Dream of the Red House*. Recently translations have appeared from French (Racine, Fournier, Simenon), Chinese (Ba Jin, Luo Guanzhong, Lao She), Japanese (Kawabata, Ariyosi Sawako), Italian (Verga, Manzoni), Russian (Chekhov, Pushkin, Strugackij), Dutch (Couperus), Spanish (Lorca), Ancient Greek (Lucian, the Gospels), Estonian (Vaarandi, Under), Romanian (Eliade) and Norwegian (Ibsen), along with translations of such English-language authors as Nevil Shute (Australia), Lewis Carroll, Oscar Wilde, Rudyard Kipling (Britain), Katherine Mansfield (New Zealand), Mark Twain, Ernest Hemingway, Edgar Allen Poe, Nathaniel Hawthorne and James Thurber (USA). In recent years, anthologies of Hungarian, German, Chinese, Korean, English, Scottish, French, Slovene, Serbian, Bulgarian, Dutch, Australian, Italian, Latin, Hebrew, Japanese, Romanian, Brazilian and Maltese literature have been published. *Asterix, Winnie-the-Pooh* and *Tin-Tin* have been joined by numerous other children's books, including, recently, *Pippi Longstocking*, and titles from China, Japan, Iceland, Israel, Sweden and Lithuania. The Internet has given children, among other things, the complete *Moomintroll* books of Finnish author Tove Jansson and the complete *Oz* books of American author L. Frank Baum.

Translation out of Esperanto:

Some works in Esperanto have been translated into other languages, including William Auld's long poem *La infana raso,* which appeared most recently (2009) in English. *Maskerado*, a memoir published in Esperanto in 1965 by Tivadar Soros, father of the financier George Soros, detailing the survival of his family during the Nazi occupation of Budapest, appeared in English translation in Britain (2000) and the United States (2001). It has been published also in Russian, German, Hungarian and Turkish translations, and an Italian translation has been announced. Dobrzynski's recent book on Zamenhof, *La Zamenhof-Strato,* has appeared in a dozen languages. A project to use Esperanto as a bridge in the translation of children's books between Croatian and Bengali is currently underway.

11

The movement to reform Esperanto

After the Boulogne congress, Zamenhof busied himself with the development of the language. In his foreword to the *Fundamento*, he had promised that he would speak in detail about the language at the Boulogne congress, but he reneged on that promise in order to avoid conflict at the congress.

Having postponed resolution of the language questions until one of the future congresses, he dealt with them in his correspondence with Javal. He outlined his ideas for the development of the language in a lengthy, 28-page letter dated September 24, 1905. He admitted that the language was not perfect. He felt, however, that the flaws were few, correctable and worth correcting because "Esperanto [had] 100–150 words or forms that were *actually* bad, and that correcting them would cause each Esperantist no more than a few hours' work to learn them once and for all, but would be of colossal benefit to Esperanto" (*Mi estas Homo*, 113). He listed the unsuitable items that were to be changed and pointed out that changing them would necessitate the introduction of *neologisms*, new words and forms that would not replace the old ones, but would exist alongside them.

Zamenhof put his project into final form and sent it to Javal on January 18, 1906. Javal was disappointed that he did not propose any change in the alphabet. In the future, argued Zamenhof, every printer and telegraph station will have the Esperanto letters and, in the meantime, "h" can be used after a letter to indicate the accent, just as the Germans use "e" to replace the umlaut. The actual changes he proposed were few: four grammatical changes and a few dozen words and affixes to replace some that were too long or were subject to misinterpretation.

Javal authored a report to the Language Committee on replacing the accented letters with non-accented ones in telegrams. He also persuaded the parliamentarian Lucien Cornet to sponsor a bill introducing Esperanto into the schools of France as an elective subject. The bill was co-sponsored by twelve other parliamentarians and was put to a vote on the April 3, 1906. It was defeated.

Javal consulted with parliamentarians and with the Committee on Public Education and wrote to Zamenhof that they would not accept Esperanto with diacritical marks and arbitrary correlative words.[11] Zamenhof replied that he would give Javal "the full right to introduce into Esperanto whatever reforms he found necessary and that [he would] publicly sign off on everything," provided Javal would guarantee the French government's acceptance of Esperanto. Javal, of course, could not give that guarantee.

The second Universal Congress of Esperanto took place in Geneva between August 27 and September 5, 1906, and passed almost without incident. The question of language reform was not dealt with in the plenary sessions and Javal's report was not even discussed. In Geneva, Javal convinced Zamenhof to study the question of reforms in a practical way and promised him 250,000 francs if he would make the changes "he thought necessary to facilitate learning the language, not only for our contemporaries, but also for future generations." The Belgian officer Charles Lemaire, founder of *Belga Sonorilo* (Belgian Bell) and president of the Royal Belgian Esperantist League, provided part of the money.

Between the October 17 and 23, 1906, a secret conference took place in Paris, involving Zamenhof, Lemaire, Javal, and two interlinguists, Miguel de Torro and André Blondel. They all wanted reforms to one extent or another, but they could not agree on how to make them, because Zamenhof, unlike the others, treated Esperanto, not as an easily changeable object, but as a living language.

Zamenhof refused the money offered, even though, at four percent interest, it would have allowed him to abandon his medical practice and live free of financial difficulties with his family. He did agree, though, that Javal and Lemaire could use a private replacement spelling and promised that he would not raise a protest if Javal published his effort. Michaux, Émile Gasse and Gaston Moch aligned themselves with the reform and Lemaire began using the proposed reforms in *Belga Sonorilo*.

Meanwhile, Professor Louis Couturat, the initiator of the Delegation for the Acceptance of an International Auxiliary Language, began corresponding with Zamenhof and various reform-minded Esperantists. The Delegation had been proposed during the Paris Exhibition in 1900 and was set up on January 17, 1901, to study the problem of international communication and to select the most suitable international language. The selection was to be made by the International Association of Academies and, if that association refused, by the Committee of the Delegation.

On November 1, 1906, Couturat circulated his project *Esperanto sen supersignoj* (Esperanto Without Accents) to Zamenhof, Javal and Michaux. Zamenhof thanked Couturat for the project, which arrived just in time to be considered in the circular *Pri neologismoj* (About Neologisms) that was to be sent to the Language Committee. Michaux approved of Couturat's reforms, but did not wish to use them without Zamenhof's approval. Javal and Lemaire both agreed with the proposals. Louis de Beaufront was interested in *Esperanto Without Accents*, although until then he had been the most anti-reformist among the influential Esperantists.

On November 22, Zamenhof sent Boirac the circular *Pri Neologismoj* for the latter to pass on to the Language Committee members. Influenced by the many recent proposals and experiments, Zamenhof had removed all accented letters from the alphabet and even promised to use the new version.

Boirac, however, refused to distribute the circular to the Committee members, who, it will be remembered, had been chosen by Zamenhof. Furthermore, Bourlet refused to publish Zamenhof's reform project in *La Revuo*. Zamenhof dropped his reform proposals, thinking that, by so doing, he was avoiding a split between the reform-minded Esperantists and the conservatives. The reformist fever had infected the Esperantists, however, and even the death of the leading reformer, Javal, on January 20, 1907, did not assuage their thirst for reform.

De Beaufront, Moch and Lemaire elaborated on Couturat's ideas. Because Zamenhof was hesitant, Couturat asked de Beaufront to pub-

The Lingva Komitato (Language Committee), 1907, in Cambridge.
L.L.Zamenhof is sitting in the first row of chairs, sixth from left.

lish his project. In May 1907, de Beaufront published Couturat's project
and signed it as "Ido" (Esperanto for "offspring"). While "Ido" was
formally de Beaufront's pseudonym, Couturat was, of course, the real
author.

Having attracted registrations from 1251 professors and academi-
cians and from 307 associations, the Delegation for the Acceptance of
an International Auxiliary Language turned to the International Association of Academies (IAA) for help in making its decision. On May
29, 1907, the IAA decided at its Vienna congress that it would not deal
with the question.

Subsequently, on June 25, the Delegation elected its own Committee. The Committee was chaired by Wilhelm Ostwald, well-known
chemist and later (1909) Nobel prize winner. The vice chairs were the
outstanding linguists Jan Niecisław Baudouin de Courtenay and Otto
Jespersen. The fourteen committee members included several linguists (Hugo Schuchardt, among others), politicians and representatives of planned languages. Couturat and Leopold Leau held office as
secretaries.

The Committee met in Paris from October 15 to 24, 1907. It defined the basic principles required of an international language – an international character (Jespersen), monosemy[12] (Ostwald), reversibility[13] (Couturat) – and tested each of the languages against them. The authors of each of the languages to be examined were invited to the session. Zamenhof delegated the "second father of Esperanto", Louis de Beaufront, to represent him.

At its final meeting on October 24, the Committee concluded that none of the languages it had examined could be accepted in its present state. Nevertheless, it did decide to accept Esperanto because of its relative state of perfection and its wide use, on condition that it be modified by the Permanent Commission in the direction defined by the conclusions of the Secretaries' Report and by the Ido project. The Commission was to make an effort to acquire the Language Committee's agreement.

The Permanent Commission began its work with Ostwald as chair, Baudouin de Courtenay, Jespersen, Couturat and Leau as members, and de Beaufront, who was co-opted "for his special competence".

The Commission's negotiations with Zamenhof and the Language Committee were not easy. Zamenhof suggested reforms several times, but only as Esperanto's author. He was not prepared to accept suggestions from others. Even Baudouin de Courtenay, who visited him in Warsaw on October 30, 1907, was unable to persuade him. Boirac had no real power, since the hundred-member Language Committee he chaired was unworkable. Ostwald, Couturat and de Beaufront had little interest in expending effort to reform Esperanto when their own language project had received recognition for its superior qualities. Additionally, the Commission was hindered because it was unclear who spoke for Esperanto; it was never sure whether it should be dealing with Zamenhof or with the Language Committee.

Zamenhof's behaviour became unstable. One day he proposed a conference to rid the language of the most serious flaws that drew constant attacks, the next day he declared the conference unnecessary. He asked Boirac to activate the Language Committee, then told him the Committee had no right to deal with an external authority, and so on. Boirac decided to resign from his position, but remained in office at Zamenhof's insistence. Finally, on January 18, 1908, Zamenhof and Boirac, in separate letters, informed Ostwald that negotiations with the Delegation were definitively broken off. No compromise was reached and, instead of an improved Esperanto, the world got yet another planned language, Ido.

The Delegation Committee's decision caused a schism among Esperantists. Approximately five percent of Esperantists converted to Ido. Up to twenty percent of the Esperanto movement's leaders were among the converted. Several periodicals and associations converted to Ido. Among the latter was the Nuremberg Club, which moved to Ido, abandoning Idiom Neutral, to which it had converted from Esperanto in 1894 after abandoning Volapük. In the May 1908 issue of *L'Espérantiste*, Louis de Beaufront identified himself as the author behind the pseudonym "Ido", and in November he resigned as president of the French Association for the Promotion of Esperanto. Despite these conversions, Idists never outnumbered Esperantists in any country and the membership of the world-wide Idist association never exceeded six hundred.

UPDATE ON ESPERANTO

Esperanto meetings:

Over 100 international conferences and meetings are held each year in Esperanto – without translators or interpreters. A list of recent venues for the annual World Congress of Esperanto shows their international character: Zagreb (2001), Fortaleza (2002), Göteborg (2003), Beijing (2004), Vilnius (2005), Florence (2006), Yokohama (2007), Rotterdam (2008), Białystok, Poland (2009), Havana (2010). Increasing regional use of Esperanto is reflected in continent-wide congresses: All-Americas Congresses occur every two or three years (e.g. Montreal 2008), as do All-Africa Congresses, and Asia Congresses (e.g. Bangalore 2008). A Middle Eastern Conference was held in Amman in 2008. There are also many meetings for Esperanto speakers at the national and local levels, which often attract participants from other countries.

12

The fruitful years

Although the Zamenhof family's circumstances improved in the years following the turn of the century, Zamenhof's life was not without problems. The revolutionary events of the years 1905–1907[14] also affected Warsaw. The conflicts among the leading Esperantists and the attacks of the Idists were poisoning Zamenhof's life. 1907 was a particularly difficult year because of the Ido schism and the deaths of both his father-in-law, Sender Zilbernik, and his father, Mark Zamenhof.

Nonetheless, on the eve of his brother's fiftieth birthday, Lev Zamenhof was able to tell the Esperanto community:

> Zamenhof's life is quiet now. He works a great deal, for his entire day is taken up by his professional work and his evenings are fully occupied with work for Esperanto. Still, despite his heavy workload and the sad state of his health (weakness of the heart and a weak pulse in the feet), he is completely happy. His only regrets are that there are not more than twenty-four hours in the day and that lack of time and poor health do not allow him to complete everything he wants to do.
>
> (*Ludovikologiaj biografietoj* 36-37)

How did he look at that time? From the recollections of contemporaries and from photos of him, we can easily recreate his appearance: He was short, always dressed in black, had dark, thinning hair and was going bald, but he had a large, greyish brown beard. His dark eyes were hidden behind gold-rimmed glasses that he never removed. He spoke gently and quietly. His

Zamenhof in 1908

movements were slow. He smoked heavily and appeared frail and unhealthy. He looked much older than he was; even when he was just in his mid-forties, he said that he felt like a man of sixty.

For almost twenty years he had lived and worked in the apartment on the second floor (the first floor in the European manner of counting) of the four-storey, redbrick house at number 19 Dzika Street. He was the only oculist in Warsaw "who devoted one day a week to free treatment for poor patients ... and on that day his home was besieged by the poor" (*Ludovikologiaj biografietoj* 86). He saw patients from Monday to Friday.

According to his nephew-in-law Max Levite, he kept the Sabbath (Maimon 36). Zamenhof's father had begun a tradition of holding family gatherings, at which friends were also welcome, in his Warsaw home on the Sabbath, and, after his death, his son carried on the tradition.

His improved financial situation enabled Zamenhof to enjoy a few weeks every summer in German spa centres: Bad Reinerz (now Duszniki-Zdrój), Bad Nauheim, Bad Kissingen, Bad Salzbrunn (now Szczawno- Zdrój), Bad Neuenahr.

His work for Hachette gave him a significant income, but in Boulogne he was forced to announce that he would no longer give his approval to the *Collection*. This required that his contract with Hachette be adjusted, but, because both sides made excessive demands, the old contract remained in force.

Bourlet, however, struck a deal with Hachette to launch a new journal with Zamenhof as a permanent contributor. For his work, Zamenhof was to receive one French franc per published line. This was an excellent deal that he could not refuse. He needed only to send ten pages a month of some translation or other of his choice in order to receive a yearly income of 4,800 francs and enjoy a good standard of living. This arrangement was also good for Esperantists, who henceforth had their first real literary journal.

The first issue of *La Revuo* appeared on September 1, 1906, with the subtitle *"Internacia monata literatura gazeto, kun la konstanta kunlabo-*

rado de D-ro L. L. Zamenhof, aŭtoro de la lingvo Esperanto" (Monthly international literary periodical with the permanent collaboration of Dr. L. L. Zamenhof, Esperanto's author). Bourlet was its editor-in-chief and its editor was Félicien Menu de Ménil, the composer of the Esperanto hymn *La Espero*. With *La Revuo* Zamenhof was freed from tedious administrative and editorial tasks, and he was no longer obliged to write insignificant texts and commentaries on the Esperanto movement.

La Revuo was founded specifically to allow him to publish his translations. The list is impressive. Most importantly, *La Revuo* published fragments of his translation of the Bible, the most widely read book in the world. *La Revuo* also published his translations of Hans Christian Andersen's *The Nightingale, The Child in the Grave,* and *The Flying Coffer;* Orzeszko's *Martha;* Shalom Aleichem's *The Grammar School;* Heine's *The Rabbi of Bacharach;* Gogol's *Revisor* (The Government Inspector); Goethe's *Iphigenia in Tauris;* Molière's *Georges Dandin;* and Schiller's *The Robbers.* All of these were later published in book form, as were Zamenhof's *Lingvaj Respondoj* (Answers to Language Questions) and *Proverbaro Esperanta* (Collection of Esperanto Proverbs).

La Revuo and *Lingvo Internacia* provided abundant information about the Universal Congresses, which Zamenhof and his wife attended every year. Both periodicals published his speeches given at the congresses.

Following the emotional speech in Boulogne, Zamenhof customarily chose some specific theme for his congress speeches. In Geneva in 1906 he wanted to present *homaranismo* (see the following chapter, "From Zionism to Homaranism"), his spiritual project for bringing together all of humankind in one human family, but was permitted to read only the first part of his written speech. In this first part he explained that, in addition to its *practical* side, Esperantism had a much more important *spiritual* side. He severely criticized Louis de Beaufront's notion that "Esperanto is *just* a language; [that Esperantists must] avoid linking Esperantism with any sort of *spiritual concept,* even in private."

> If we, Esperanto's first defenders, are forced to avoid every-
> thing spiritual in our activity, we will indignantly tear up and
> burn everything we have written for Esperanto, we will pain-
> fully undo the work and sacrifices of our whole lives, we will
> hurl from us the green stars we wear on our breasts, and we
> will shout with loathing, "We will have nothing to do with
> *that* sort of Esperanto, an Esperanto forced into the exclusive
> service of commerce and practicality."
>
> (*Mi estas Homo* 171)

At the opening of the third Universal Congress, held in Cambridge in 1907, Zamenhof spoke about the essence and goal of the Esperanto congresses. Following the congress, he gave a public speech in the City of London's Guildhall, in which he responded to two accusations; first, that Esperantists oppose improving the language and, second, that Esperantists are not patriotic.

Dresden was the host city for the fourth Universal Congress, in 1908. Because of the schism caused by Ido, Zamenhof devoted his speech to the theme of the stability and development of Esperanto and to the role of the Language Committee. At the Dresden congress, the Esperanto Academy (*Akademio de Esperanto*), with Boirac as chairman, was chosen to be the upper chamber of the Language Committee. The Dresden congress also saw the first meeting of the Universal Esperanto Association (*Universala Esperanto-Asocio*), founded in Geneva on April 28, 1908. UEA's first president was the Briton Harold Bolingbroke Mudie. The Swiss Hector Hodler was its vice president and editor of the journal *Esperanto*.

The fifth Universal Congress was held in Barcelona from September 5 to 11, 1909, under the protection of King Alfonso XIII of Spain. Unfortunately, this royal protection, and the king's post-congress proclamation of Zamenhof as a commander of the Order of Isabella the Catholic, made an unfavourable impression on those who sympathized with the victims of the brutally suppressed Barcelona revolt of the previous July. Zamenhof did not even touch on the subject of the revolt in his Barcelona address, which was the least important of all his congress speeches.

In 1910, the Universal Congress was held outside Europe for the first time, in Washington, DC. It was Zamenhof's first trip outside Europe and he found himself in the country where, almost thirty years earlier, he had advocated creating a Jewish homeland. He began his opening address to the Sixth Congress with much pathos:

> Land of freedom, land of the future, I salute you! Land that the suffering and innocently persecuted masses have dreamt of and dream of still, I salute you! Kingdom of humanity, belonging, not to this or that people or church, but to all your honest children, I bow down before you.
>
> (*Mi estas Homo* 188)

With less passion, he addressed the question, "Does our work set us on a truly sure path, or must we fear that all our labours will some day prove to have been in vain?" He maintained that he had already answered that question in his article *Essence and Future* and that he was not just presenting a summary of that text.

After the Washington congress, Zamenhof and Sébert produced the rules that were to govern future congresses. According to these rules, only the "regularly elected delegates from Esperanto groups and associations" with more than twenty-five paid-up members registered at the Central Office, the *Rajtigitaj Delegitoj* (Authorized Delegates), would have the right to vote at the congresses. Zamenhof made this project the subject of his speech at the seventh congress in Antwerp (1911). In Antwerp, the creation of the Authorized Delegates was approved by the Authorized Delegates themselves, and the ordinary congress participants lost the right to vote at the Universal Congresses.

The eighth Universal Congress took place in Cracow in 1912 and had as its theme the quarter-century anniversary of Esperanto. At this congress, Zamenhof announced that he was giving up any role in Esperanto so that his political and religious ideas would not be considered those of the Esperanto movement.

Although Zamenhof had often spoken of the congresses as celebrations, they were tiring for him. According to his brother Lev, even during the first congresses he was ill with arteriosclerosis and each congress caused his health to deteriorate further. Lev wrote that being present during the congresses was for Zamenhof "not a joyous triumph, but a painful duty." The first two congresses, during which he suffered the bullying of the leading Parisian Esperantists, demanded enormous amounts of nervous energy from him.

The jubilee congress in Cracow was also difficult. Having learned that the Local Congress Committee was planning to honour him in Cracow, he asked that it not do so. The reason for his request was that articles often appeared in Poland denouncing Esperanto. These negative articles were different from those of other countries, however, because instead of criticizing the idea or the language, they were directed against Zamenhof himself, whose faults were that he was a Jew and he was born in Litva. He knew that honouring him would incite Polish patriots, who rejected Esperanto as having been created by a Litvak. He asked also that he not be identified as a Pole, so that Polish nationalists would not be able to claim that he had adopted the guise of a nation to which he did not belong in order to receive an honour.

After the Cracow congress, Zamenhof was attacked anyway, but by Jewish patriots, because of an episode during the congress in which he had not supported a proposal by the Jewish participants to bring greetings to the congress in the name of the Jewish people. Jewish journalists took note of this and criticized Zamenhof in two post-congress articles: *La juda demando en kongreso de Esperanto* (The Jewish Question at the Congress of Esperanto) by Dov Ber Borochov in *Di Varhajt* (The Truth) (September 15, 1912) and *Skandalo ĉe Esperantista kongreso* (Scandal at the Congress of Esperantists) published anonymously in *Togblat* (Daily Paper) in Lvov (August 16, 1912). Zamenhof had to publish a response to *Di Varhajt* in order to disavow the statement the paper had attributed to him: "In order not to damage Esperanto, I have to hide my Jewishness." In his response, he wrote:

> Every Esperantist in the world knows full well that I am a Jew, because I have never hidden the fact, although I do not shout it chauvinistically from the rooftops. Esperantists know that I have translated texts from the Yiddish language; they know that for more than three years I have devoted all my free time to translating the Bible from the Hebrew original; they know that I have always lived in an exclusively Jewish quarter of Warsaw (where many Jews are ashamed to live); they know that I have always had my works printed by a Jewish printer, etc. Are these the acts of someone who is ashamed of his origins and who is trying to hide his Jewishness?
>
> (*Mi estas Homo* 201)

UPDATE ON ESPERANTO

Professional contacts among Esperanto speakers:

Professional organizations for Esperanto speakers include associations for doctors and medical workers, writers, railway workers, scientists, mathematicians, astronomers, and musicians. Such organizations often publish their own journals, hold conferences and help to expand the language for professional and specialized use. The International Academy of Sciences of San Marino, which teaches in Esperanto, has established its own system of courses and diplomas. There is a steady flow of original and translated publications in such fields as astronomy, computing, botany, entomology, chemistry, law and philosophy. The Centre for Research and Documentation on World Language Problems brings linguists and social scientists together around the study of communication across languages and its journal *Language Problems and Language Planning* includes a section on interlinguistics, the study of the conditions for planned international language.

13

From Zionism to Homaranism

In addition to his theoretical work on Yiddish grammar, Zamenhof had devoted time and energy during his student years to the question of the future of the Jews. He later (1905) wrote to Alfred Michaux that, when he was at university, he was "a keen Zionist" and "successfully founded the first Zionist groups" (*Mi estas Homo* 101). He provided further details of this activity in an interview he gave to the London newspaper *The Jewish Chronicle* in 1907:

> I have always had a strong interest in the social life of my people and, in my youth, I was a keen political Zionist. That was many years before Herzl appeared on the scene and before the idea of a Jewish state became popular among Jews. As early as 1881, while I was a university student in Moscow, I held a meeting with fifteen of my fellow students and put forward a plan that I had thought out. According to my plan, we would found a Jewish colony in some unpopulated part of the world. This colony would represent the beginning and would become the centre of an independent Jewish state. I was able to convince my fellow students and we formed something that was, or so I believe, the first Jewish political organization in Russia.

When Zamenhof graduated from university in 1884, a controversy was raging in the Jewish press over the future of Russia's Jews. The newspaper *Razsvet* often suggested emigration to the United States, Spain, Palestine, or Argentina, but the rival papers *Russkij Jevrej* and *Voshiod* were critical of these proposals and advocated seeking a solution within Russia to the problem facing the Russian Jews.

The twenty-two-year-old Zamenhof was a participant in the discussion about emigration in *Razsvet*. In January and February 1882, in issues 2, 3, 4, and 5, his lengthy article *What Action Should We Ultimately Take?* was published under the name Gamzefon (*Mi estas homo* 5-22). In this article, Zamenhof advocated mass emigration of the Jews and examined both Palestine and the United States as potential destinations. He argued against Palestine where he felt the Jews would encounter hostile Christians, Turks and "wild, fanatical robber groups living in Palestine and the surrounding regions and thumbing their noses at any authority." He proposed instead that the Jews emigrate to some sparsely populated territory of the United States, attract Jews there from around the world and declare the territory a Jewish state within the framework of the United States.

In the debate over whether to choose the United States or Palestine, Zamenhof finally joined the supporters of the Palestine solution "in order not to fragment himself" and published the article, *Under a Common Flag!* (1882) in which he made an emotional concluding appeal:

> The way lies open before us and the goal is clearly defined. Let us colonize Palestine and unite our people in the ancient homeland, family after family, group after group.... Let us pay the Arab twice or three times its value and he will sell us as much land as you need; a golden key will easily open every Turkish chancery.... Like bees from flowers and plants, we will succeed in bringing into our country divers traits drop by drop, one drop at a time. Through concerted action, we will succeed in returning life and glory to the land. Every wealthy person who settles there will perform thereby a great service for his people; every school founded there will be a step forward toward the clearest goal.... Let us join together, brothers, let us rise up beneath the only flag capable of uniting us! On that flag is written the one word "Homeward!"
>
> (*Mi estas Homo* 26)

Zamenhof became active in the Chibat Zion (Love of Zion) movement, whose aim was to found agricultural colonies in Palestine. Chibat Zion's members were called Chovevey Zion (Lovers of Zion) and, later, the movement itself adopted the same name. In February 1882, Zamenhof founded and led the student society Shearith Israel in Warsaw. He wrote the bylaws, had them printed and distributed them, organized meetings, concerts and dances, recruited members and set up a Jewish library. He also collected contributions from different groups for colonies in Palestine and sent them on to Germany.

Shearith Israel and the general association of Chibat Zion merged in August 1883 and the twenty-three-year-old Zamenhof chaired the Warsaw group's action committee. One of his responsibilities in that role was to stay in touch with the Bilu activists, a socialist youth group belonging to Chibat Zion who went to Palestine and began work there. Zamenhof himself intended to go to Palestine but decided to finish his university studies first.

Gradually, though, Zamenhof's Zionist activism diminished. He did not attend the first conference of Chibat Zion in Kattowitz in 1884 and once he received his medical degree at the end of that year he was only a passive observer of Jewish social activism. Yet although his active involvement ended, he did not stop looking for a solution to the Jewish question. After seventeen years of reflection, he published his thoughts in January 1901 in a 78-page book, *Gillelizm. Projekt rešenija jevrejskogo voprosa* (Hillelism: A Plan for Solving the Jewish Problem). The book was published under the pseudonym Homo Sum, Latin for "I am a human being."

Since this text is a key to understanding Zamenhof's philosophy, it is worth taking some time to understand the background.

The name *Hillelism* alludes to the rabbi Hillel, who presided over the Jewish tribunal in the time of Herod. A number of his pronouncements are found in the Talmud, including the Golden Rule, in which he summed up God's laws: "Do not do unto others that which is hateful to you. Therein lies the entire Law; all the rest is mere commentary."

The situation of the Jews in Russia had changed by the end of the nineteenth century. In his two articles for *Razsvet*, written twenty years before *Hillelism*, Zamenhof talked about the Jews of the previous era, who were mostly small merchants, middlemen, tradespeople, factory owners. There were almost no capitalists and highly educated scholars among them. By the beginning of the twentieth century, however, there were several Jews among the major capitalists and bankers. The most drastic change, though, was in the intellectual sphere. For centuries the Jewish *kahals*, or governing councils, had resisted the government's attempts to provide Jews with a secular education, with the result that Jews still received a traditional *cheder* education in Hebrew and Jewish religion, which was of little use in the professions. Little by little, however, the influence of the leaders of the *cheders* and of the rabbis diminished and Jews began to study in Gymnasiums and universities in great numbers.

Although Jews comprised less than four percent of Russia's population, they represented 14.5% of the students in Russian universities in 1887 and, despite the limits on their numbers imposed later, they still made up 12.1% of university students prior to the 1917 revolution. Furthermore, many Jews – including also Zamenhof's children Adam and Sofia later on – attended foreign universities. Consequently, many university-educated Jews appeared in Russia: cultural activists, scientists, physicians, financiers, lawyers, and so on. These intellectuals lived mostly in Petersburg, Moscow and large administrative district capitals beyond the border regions of eastern Russia. They spoke the Russian language and had little connection with the old-style small-merchant Jews. As first- or second-generation intellectuals, however, they had still not fully assimilated into Russian society.

Chibat Zion's activity gradually lost its influence among the Russian Jews. Poor Jews still migrated to the United States, but there was very little migration to Palestine. In his 1896 book *The Jewish State: An Attempt at a Modern Solution to the Jewish Question*, the Austrian Jew Theodor (Binjamin Zeev) Herzl proposed founding an independent Jewish state not through gradual emigration, but through the political decision of major governments. Adhering to the concept of *The Jewish State*, the first Zionist Congress (Basel, 1897) adopted the programme of the Zionist movement and founded the World Zionist Organization with Herzl as chairman.

Several theoretical solutions to the Jewish problem were generally known:

- **Assimilation** is the absorption of the Jews into the majority group in their country through gradual linguistic and cultural identification and through mixed marriages, whose offspring consider themselves members of the majority group. In earlier times the assimilated Jews kept their religion, but, beginning in the twentieth century, they also lost their religion and considered their national identity to be much more important than their ethnic or religious one.

- **Zionism** involves the creation of a separate Jewish state to which Jews from all over the world would come in order to the majority group with all the majority's privileges and duties.

- **Autonomism** means living in a Jewish diaspora in autonomous ethnic-cultural groups that differ according to the country in which they live. The theory of autonomism was defined by the Russian Jew Simeon Markovitch Dubnov in the years 1897 to 1902. According to his theory, the whole world is the Jewish homeland, because the Jewish people is the first to have arrived at the highest level of existence, at which the Jews no longer need their religious traditions expressed in the Hebrew language, but only their culture and spirit expressed in Yiddish.

- Other proposals for the solution to the Jewish problem include the assimilation of other ethnic groups by the Jews, assigning to Jews the status of foreigners with a corresponding absence of responsibilities and rights, and the "final solution" carried out by the Nazis.

In 1901 Zamenhof dealt only with assimilation and Zionism.

Assimilation is not a suitable solution, he argued, because the majority group does not accept the Jews as equals, even if the Jews have the same names and speak the same language as themselves. Zamenhof judged the assimilationist formula, "we are Frenchmen/women, Germans, Poles, etc. with a Mosaic religion," to be a compromise based on sophistry and falsehood and rejected by the majority group. The first part of the formula is a falsehood because Jews are Jews and not

Frenchmen/women, Germans and Poles. The second part is inexact because there cannot be Frenchmen/women, Germans and Poles with the Mosaic religion, which is reserved exclusively for Jews. Even if this formula were true, Zamenhof argued, educated Jews are not religious and so do not meet the criterion of having the Mosaic religion.

Next, Zamenhof analyzes the Zionist idea: "We are not Frenchmen/women, Germans, Poles, etc., but Jews, not only by religion but also ethnically. Therefore, we must strive for independence in Palestine."

Against this idea, Zamenhof attempts to prove that it is only a tradition to call the Jews a people. For him, a people is a human group that lives in a given territory, speaks the same language, practises the same religion, and has political independence. Jews, he maintains, meet only the religious criterion and therefore cannot be a people. They do not even have the same language. Hebrew was spoken in antiquity and later served as the language of religion, but it is as foreign and difficult for Jews as it is for non-Jews. As for Yiddish, it is spoken only by some of the Eastern-European Jews.

Having rejected the Zionist thesis, Zamenhof explains that the Jewish state cannot be built in Palestine for three reasons:

1. Palestine is administered by Turkey, which will never permit an independent state to be created on its territory.

2. Even if the proposed state could be built, its territory would be too small. No more than a million Jews would be able to immigrate to it, while the remaining nine million would remain in the countries they now inhabit. Furthermore, the situation of the nine million would become worse, because the antisemitic majorities would consider them even more foreign than before and would have a moral basis to shout, "Go to your Palestine!"

3. Despite Turkey's administration of it, Palestine belongs and will continue to belong to the powerful Christian world, which has its most holy places throughout there. The presence of these holy places will cause eternal conflict with Christians.

What, then, is the solution to the Jewish problem? To solve the problem, we must know its causes. According to the Zionists, the main cause is the two-thousand-year exile, but Zamenhof believed that the Jews' specific situation was caused not by the loss of their land and independence, losses experienced by all ancient peoples, but rather by the merging of ethnicity with religion. Because of this merging of two identities into one, the Jews can neither be absorbed into another ethnic group nor themselves absorb different peoples. The Jews remain an abnormal people, despised by every other.

Christianity, Islam and Buddhism are open to all ethnicities, argued Zamenhof. They do not have the ethnic character of Judaism, which favours only one chosen people. This discriminates against the other peoples. Therefore, it is necessary to change the Hebrew religion and remove from it everything ethnic. Because it is not possible to quickly change the religion of ten million people, however, Zamenhof proposed that a small Hillel community should be founded first and that it would later absorb all Jews.

Hillelism is therefore a religious fraction in the heart of the Hebrew religion, but freed from the incidental admixture that had long made it an anachronism. It is interpreted not according to the strict letter of the words of Moses, but rather in accordance with their spirit, which can be formulated in a few basic principles:

1.   We feel and acknowledge the existence of the highest Force that rules the world, and we name this Force God.

2.   God placed his laws in every person's heart in the form of the conscience. Always obey the voice of your conscience, therefore, because it is the never silent voice of God.

3.   The essence of all laws given to us by God can be expressed by the following formula: Love thy neighbour and do unto others as you would have them do unto you and never commit acts openly or in secret that your inner voice tells you would not be pleasing to God. All other instructions that you may hear from your teachers

and leaders and that do not fit into the three main points of religion are merely human commentaries, which could be true, but which could also be false.

The Hillel temple will always be a temple of pure philosophy so that questions about the "high Force," about morality, about life and death, about the human body and spirit, and so on, can be freely discussed and studied. As the language of communication, education and liturgy, Homo Sum proposed Esperanto.

This Hillel group, with its purified religion and Esperanto, is to choose a place to which will come all Jews who decide to emigrate from their normal homeland and who wish to live among their own kind.

The final goal of Hillelism is to integrate the Jew with the peoples of the whole world:

> Through our ideas we can acquire the whole civilized world, just as the Christians have succeeded in doing until now, even though they began as a small group of Hebrews. Instead of being absorbed into the Christian world, we will absorb it.
>
> (*Mi estas Homo* 253)

Zamenhof distributed his book to "a small number of intelligent Jews" and presented it at one of the "Monday meetings" at Nahum Sokolov's house,[15] but he received few reactions. In fact, history has shown that Zamenhof was on the wrong track:

- the assimilationists found their solution in emigration to the United States;

- the Zionists won with the creation of Israel;

- the chief obstacle to the Jews in Palestine became Islam rather than Christianity;

- the ancient Hebrew language became a spoken language adapted to the needs of modern life;

- the ancient Hebrew religion became the official religion of Israel.

Zamenhof had another goal that he did not reveal to the Jews. He needed a stable social base for Esperanto, which otherwise could disappear, as Volapük had. In his own words:

> An international language will become forever strong only if there exists a group of people who accept it as their family, *hereditary* language. One hundred such people are hugely more important to the idea of a neutral language than a million other people. The hereditary language of even the smallest and most insignificant human group has a much stronger guarantee of a continued existence than a language without a people even if it is used by millions.
>
> (Letter to Kofman 1901: *Mi estas Homo* 97)

Zamenhof wavered, however, on the question of the composition of his neutral people. Several years later, he said of his hesitation:

> In the course of time, I have arrived at the strong conviction that the first group of Hillelists should not be multicultural, but should be an ethnically homogeneous group that will add a Hillelist character to its own existing traditions and ideals. In this way, acting as a sect, it will form a hereditary, existing and historically-based group that will engulf first its own people, then the whole of humanity. Only one group can do this, namely the Hebrew people. Not until I have decided definitively to reject the idea of Hebrew Hillelism will I propose in one of the Esperanto congresses the creation of multicultural, Esperanto-speaking Hillelists.
>
> (Letter to Javal 1905: *Mi estas Homo* 119)

14

Esperanto and the brotherhood of humanity

The phrase Zamenhof used in Boulogne concerning "the creation of a brotherhood of human beings from diverse ethnic groups" and his poetic call for the unity of all religions, which was censored by the atheistic French leadership, alluded to the project he wrote to Javal about after returning home from the congress:

> This project, which I intend to show to the world sooner or later under the name of "Hillelism" is the most important of all the work I have ever done or will ever do. In itself, it presents in full fruition the idea to which I have devoted my entire life; the whole Esperanto project is only a *part* of this common idea, which I call Hillelism.
>
> (Letter to Javal, 1905: *Mi estas Homo* 115-116)

The project's strategic goal was the unification of humanity, but the tactical objective was the creation of a neutrally human population, whose members would be separated from each other by geographical and political boundaries, but not by their languages or their religions.

Zamenhof's concept had taken shape under the influence of Russian spiritual Zionism, which rejected the need for a separate Jewish state and argued that having the cultural centre of Judaism in Palestine would be sufficient. Zamenhof adapted this ideology to his doctrine in the following way:

> The Hillelists will proceed in the following manner: they will choose a specific city in neutral Switzerland, which will become forever the spiritual centre for all Hillelists in the world. In that city there will be a permanent central committee of Hillelists; it will also house the central Hillelist temple, in which

every human being will be able to serve the mysterious Moral Force that rules the world.... Of course, only a *neutrally human* language and morals will reign in the Hillelist temple.

(Letter to Javal, 1905: *Mi estas Homo* 118)

According to Zamenhof's plan, the first Hillelist sect was to be exclusively Jewish, but the success of the Boulogne congress changed his plan, so that he intended to announce at the second Universal Congress of Esperanto (in Geneva, 1906) that the first Hillelist group was to be made up of Esperantists.

Because of the increasing tension of the revolutionary situation in Russia, however, Zamenhof decided to publish his ideas before the Geneva congress took place. In the January 1906 issue of *Ruslanda Esperantisto* (Russian Esperantist), he published his doctrine anonymously under the title *Dogmoj de Hilelismo* (Beliefs of Hillelism) with parallel Russian and Esperanto texts.

The foreword makes it clear that, first, Hillelism was a response to a particular, concrete situation in Russia; second, it presented that situation not as a class struggle, but as an ethnic, religious and linguistic conflict, and, third, it was too closely associated with Esperanto.

Following the foreword, Zamenhof defined the essence and goal of Hillelism and the twelve beliefs of the *Hillelist's Declaration*. The lay version of *Hillelism*, aimed at Russians and Esperantists, is very different from the 1901 project, which had the same name but was intended specifically for Jews. The earlier project had been a purified version of the Hebrew religion. The new project was another thing entirely:

Hillelism is a doctrine that, without tearing a person away from his native country, or language, or religion, gives him the possibility of avoiding all untruths or contradictions in the principles of his national religion, and of communicating with people of all languages and religions on a neutrally human basis, according to principles of mutual brotherhood, equal-

> ity and justice.... Hillelists hope that, through constant mutual
> communication based on a neutral language and on neutral
> religious principles and customs, humanity will some day be
> united as one neutrally human people.
>
> (*Beliefs of Hillelism*, 1906: *Mi estas Homo* 130)

The first four beliefs are the most general and most clearly reflect *Hillelism*'s basic principles:

1. I am a human being, and for me only purely human ideals exist. I consider any ethnic or national ideals to be nothing but group egotism and hatred for others. These ethnic and national ideals are destined to disappear sooner or later and I must hasten their disappearance in so far as I am able.

2. I believe that all peoples are equal and I judge each individual on his personal value and actions, not on his origin. I consider any offensive action or persecution directed towards a person simply because he was born into a different ethnicity with a different language or religion from mine to be an act of barbarism.

3. I believe that every country belongs, not to this or that people, but to all its inhabitants, with full and equal rights, regardless of their language or religion. The mixing of national interests with those of this or that people, language or religion I see as a remnant of the barbaric times when only might was right.

4. I believe that, in their family life, all people have a full, natural and indisputable right to speak whatever language or dialect and to practise whichever religion they please, but that when communicating with people of different origins, they should, in so far as it is possible, use a neutrally human language and live according to the principles of a neutrally human religion. I regard as an act of barbarism any attempt by a person to impose his language or religion on others.

Zamenhof then explained the differences between a "sovereign state" (*regno*), a "country" (*lando*) and a "fatherland" (*patrujo*), and urged the use of only geographically neutral names for countries, such as Austria, Belgium, Switzerland, Canada, Mexico, etc. Names of countries formed from the name of their majority ethnic group should be changed. Thus, he suggested the use of "Parisian State" (Parizregno) instead of France (*Francio*), "Petersburg State" (*Peterburgregno*) instead of Russia, and "Warsawland" (*Varsovilando*) instead of Poland, because the nationalistic and ethnic basis of the traditional country names – *Francs, Russians, Poles* – would discriminate against all other inhabitants of those countries.

In these sovereign states and countries with neutral names, no single group of people would impose their language and religion on their fellow inhabitants, and communication between groups would be through a neutrally human language. Festivals would not celebrate ethnicity or religion, but only common humanity or citizenship. In the sovereign states there would be no ethnic groups, only individuals and citizens.

The ninth belief recommends that the Hillelist language, in other words, Esperanto, be used and that the mother tongue be called, not the *national*, but the *family* language.

The tenth belief outlines the religious principles of Hillelism:

- By the name "God", I mean that highest Force, incomprehensible to me, that rules the world and whose essence I have the right to interpret for myself as my wisdom and feelings dictate.

- The foundation of my religion I consider to be the rule "Do unto others as you would have them do unto you, and always listen to the voice of your conscience." Everything else is tradition or custom introduced by human beings.

- Because the essence of every traditional religion is the same, and they are differentiated only by traditions and customs, the diverse religious customs of each Hillelist are to give way to common, neutrally human customs.

The eleventh belief relates to the Hillelist temples, where Hillelists from various religions are to gather in order to develop a "philosophically pure, but at the same time beautiful, poetic, warm and life-governing religion that will be common to all humans and that parents can transmit to their children without pretense."

Nothing is known of the reaction of non-Esperantists to Zamenhof's project, but the Esperantists rejected it. Non-Jews disliked its Talmudic name. Atheists found it too religious. It seemed heretical to those with religious faith. Those engaged in class conflict judged it politically misguided. Outsiders did not understand the particular Russian circumstances.

Zamenhof realized that he had given the doctrine too Jewish a name and that his foreword was oriented too much towards the Russian situation. Consequently, in March there appeared in Petersburg the booklet entitled *Homaranism* (literally: *Humanityism*). He emphasized in the new foreword that, whereas *Hillelism* had affected only one group of people, *Homaranism* affected all peoples and religions. The name and the foreword had changed, but the difference between the January and the March projects was nearly all terminological: instead of Hillelists, it was now a question of *Homaranists*, or "members of the human race", and instead of "Petersburg State" (*Petersburgregno*), it was now "Petersburgland" (*Petersburgio*).

Nothing positive appeared in the Esperantist press, but there were two critical commentaries, one from a Lithuanian Roman Catholic priest, Alexander Dambrauskas, and one by Louis de Beaufront. Javal and Sebert also rejected *Homaranism* and advised Zamenhof to hide the fact that he was its author, for fear of causing a schism in the Esperanto movement.[16]

Zamenhof intended to launch *Homaranism* at the Geneva congress and also to launch the first *Homaranist* community there. However, Javal and Sebert, to whom Zamenhof had sent the text of his congress speech for approval, persuaded him not to read the second part of the speech, in which he identified the "internal idea" of Esperanto with *Homaranism*. Zamenhof gave in. Almost no one knew that Zamenhof had read just the beginning of his speech in Geneva. For this reason, the "internal idea", mentioned in the first part of the speech, but presented in detail in the second part, later received conflicting interpretations.

Zamenhof realized that, despite the euphoria at the Boulogne congress, the Esperantists were not prepared to accept *Homaranism* and "to reunite humanity". Indeed, even Javal and Michaux, his two closest Esperantist collaborators, tried to persuade him not to link Esperanto with any religious doctrine. For some time, therefore, he avoided any public mention of *Homaranism* and preferred instead to speak of the vague "internal idea", which was, in a sense, a surrogate for *Homaranism*.

Born, brought up and educated in multicultural Russia, Zamenhof failed to realize that in Germany, France and many other Western-European countries multilingualism barely existed and that religion no longer played its earlier role. Because he concentrated too strongly on language and religion, he barely took note of the existence of the political, economic and psychological factors.

UPDATE ON ESPERANTO

Esperanto periodicals:

More than a hundred magazines and journals are published regularly in Esperanto, including the news magazine *Monato* and UEA's monthly journal *Esperanto*. Electronic journals include *Libera Folio,* the principal source of information and opinion on the Esperanto movement itself. Among other periodicals are scholarly publications in medicine and science, religious magazines, national Esperanto journals, periodicals for young people, educational periodicals, literary magazines, and numerous special-interest publications.

15

Spirituality and Esperanto

Having divested himself of his official role in Esperanto at the Universal Congress in Cracow, Zamenhof could transfer his activity to the ideological sphere. A little more than a year previously, in late 1910, he had written a speech in Esperanto for the First Universal Races Congress in London, *Gentoj kaj Lingvo Internacia* (Peoples and the International Language).

Zamenhof believed that interracial divisions and hatred were not caused by political, economic, geographic, anatomical, or intellectual differences, or by different origins. The main cause, he argued in his speech, was difference in language and religion. Therefore, "The diversity of peoples and the hatred of each other which they betray will not wholly disappear from the face of the earth until humanity has but one language and one religion."(International Language 430)

Because the creation of a unified human race was not possible in the near future, however, humanity should organize itself in such a way that "while preserving their national language and religion in the internal life of their linguistic or religious groups, men shall, in their relations with other peoples, use a language that is neutral to all men, and live according to the rules of a moral code which dictates actions and customs that are similarly neutral" (International Language 431). Without treating the religious theme in detail, Zamenhof argued for the use of Esperanto. He did not attend the congress, which took place from July 26 to 29, 1911, with 3,000 participants, but his speech was published in the imposing proceedings of the congress (International Language 425-432).

Having shown the way to dispel linguistic divisions, Zamenhof presented, after the Cracow congress, the solution to religious differences. In 1913, he planned to organize a Congress for a Neutrally Human Religion in conjunction with the Tenth Universal Congress of Esperanto to be held in Paris the following year. His idea was unusual: he intended to address, not those who believed their religion was the only true one given by God, but freethinkers who had abandoned the religion of their forefathers. Of the four theses expressed in his Declaration, three were more or less in line with the religious dogmas of *Homaranism*, while the fourth dealt with organization. The Parisian leaders of the Esperanto movement opposed his plan, so he decided to hold a separate, small congress in Bern following the Esperanto Congress in Paris.

In the same year, he published a new version of the *Declaration of Homaranism* and, for the first time, signed it with his real name. The text was changed somewhat, especially in the religious part, where the temples were no longer mentioned, but communities of freethinkers were added. The concrete, neutrally human names of countries no longer figured in the text. Mentions of Russia and the Boulogne congress were deleted from the foreword. Zamenhof accepted that, within a state or city, the role of neutral language could be filled by the official language or by the "cultural language spoken by the majority of the local population" and that the neutrally human language was recommended for those places where different ethnic groups were in conflict with each other.

At the Ninth Universal Congress in Bern in 1913, Zamenhof was for the first time just a simple congress participant. The keynote speech was delivered by the Swiss scientist René de Saussure, brother of the famous linguist Ferdinand de Saussure.

Two weeks before the Bern congress, on August 12, 1913, Carlo Bourlet passed away. Bourlet's death was a severe blow, because without his influence, Hachette lost interest in Esperanto and the eighth volume of *La Revuo* (September 1913–August 1914) turned out to be the last. Zamenhof quickly realized that in August 1914 he would lose his main source of income and that he would not be able to publish his Biblical texts with Hachette. He looked for a new publisher. Finally, he reached an agreement to publish his translation of the Old Testament with the British and Foreign Bible Society.

Because the translation of the Old Testament took all his free time, he set aside almost everything else related to Esperanto. We will mention only two events in which he was obliged to intervene.

First, in 1914, it was suggested to Zamenhof that he become a member of the Hebrew Esperanto Association, whose founding meeting was to take place during the Paris Congress. Zamenhof approved of the association's founding, but, as a *Homaranist*, he did not want to ally himself with any ethnic group or religion. He explained his decision as follows:

> I am deeply convinced that all nationalism represents nothing but the greatest misfortune for humanity and that every human being should strive to create harmony within the human race, whose only boundaries should be geographical, not racial or religious. It is true that the nationalism of oppressed peoples, which is a natural reaction of self-defence, is much more forgivable than that of their oppressors. Nevertheless, if the nationalism of the powerful is ignoble, that of the weak is imprudent, for they each give rise to and sustain each other and represent a vicious circle of misery, from which humanity will never escape unless all of us sacrifice our group egotism and make an effort to stand on completely *neutral* ground.
>
> That is the reason why, despite the heart-rending sufferings of my people, I will not ally myself with Hebrew nationalism, but prefer to work only for *absolute* justice between peoples. I am profoundly convinced that I can do much more good for my unhappy race in this way than by nationalistic endeavours.
>
> (*Mi estas Homo* 217-218)

Second, anti-Semitism was increasing in Poland. It even permeated the journal *Pola Esperantisto* (Polish Esperantist), which published in its May 1914 issue the article "Poloj kaj hebreoj" by Andrzej Niemojewski, a Polish author, translator and scientist, who was also an Esperantist. It was not the article itself that most distressed Zamenhof, for similar articles were common in Poland. What upset him the most was the foreword by *Pola Esperantisto*'s editor, the Warsaw journalist Mieczysław

Czerwiński, who called the Talmud "a horrible book of superstitions and hatred of everything non-Jewish."

Zamenhof sent a protest to *Pola Esperantisto*. Czerwiński did not publish it and, instead, mentioned in the June issue that the editor had received several protests from Jews who "clearly revealed to us the lack of education of those who defend the Talmud". At the same time, he declared open war on the Talmud.

Radio and television:

Radio stations, both free-air and internet, in Brazil, China, Cuba, Korea, Poland, and many other countries broadcast regularly in Esperanto, as does Vatican Radio. Television stations broadcast occasional reports in or on Esperanto, including the local television station in Białystok, Poland, birthplace of the author of Esperanto, Zamenhof.

Internet:

Electronic networks are the fastest-growing means of communication among Esperanto speakers. There are hundreds of special-interest lists in Esperanto, for discussion of topics ranging from the family use of the language to the general theory of relativity. The number of websites and blogs in Esperanto is unknown, but certainly runs into the thousands. Among the most popular is *www.lernu.net*, a site for learning Esperanto and networking with new speakers. The site *www.uea.org* offers access to the Universal Esperanto Association's bookstore and to much additional information. The site *www.esperantic.org* gives information in English on Esperanto studies.

16

The First World War

A few weeks after this journalistic declaration of war against the Jews, another war was declared: the First World War. On his way to the Universal Congress in Paris with his wife, Zamenhof was stopped in Germany and, as citizens of Russia, an enemy state, the Zamenhofs had to spend two weeks making a roundabout trip through Scandinavia and Petersburg in order to return to Warsaw. The Paris Congress never took place.

Because of the war, the neutrally human religion congress was also postponed, although, on September 9, 1914, Zamenhof approached the Swiss Esperantist and freemason Friedrich Uhlmann with the suggestion that he organize a congress in Switzerland in 1915 and invite participation not only from Esperantists, but from every person who aspired to the unification of humanity. Uhlmann advised him to get in touch with René de Saussure. Consequently, on October 18 Zamenhof sent Saussure his plan for the Congress on a Neutrally Human Religion, whose goal was to establish a set of new religious principles for all people who had lost their traditional religious faith yet still yearned to belong to some religious community, and to found a community for such people.

In late 1914, Zamenhof composed his call to diplomats, *Post la granda milito* (After the Great War) and sent it to several Esperantist publications for them to publish in Esperanto and in national languages. He foresaw that the diplomats would reshape the map of Europe after the war and he proposed the creation of a United States of Europe. Realizing, however, that this proposal could not become reality, he asked the diplomats at least to proclaim and guarantee in every sovereign European state the principle that "Every country belongs, both morally and materially and with full rights, to all its children." Finally, he recommended that the future peace conference institute the following laws:

1. Each sovereign state shall belong morally and materially to all its natural and naturalized inhabitants regardless of their language, religion or supposed origin. No ethnic group in the state shall have greater or lesser rights than the other groups.

2. All citizens shall have the full right to use whatever language or dialect and to practise whatever religion they please. Whichever language is accepted by common consent of the citizens to be the state's official language shall be used only in public institutions that are not designed to serve one particular ethnic group.

3. For all injustices committed in a given state, the government of that state shall be answerable to a Permanent Pan-European Tribunal created by mutual agreement of all European states.

4. Every sovereign state and every province shall bear, not the name of some ethnic group, but a neutrally geographic name adopted by common consent of all states. (After the Great War, 1915: *Mi estas Homo* 232)

Once his call to diplomats was completed, Zamenhof worked on a project to "revise Esperanto once and for all", because there were still unsuitable elements in the language that he had not noticed when he had been developing it prior to its publication. He felt that the 28-year practical functioning of the language was sufficient to reveal any problems with the language and that "problems that [had] not been found in the language by now will never be found in it."

Zamenhof was afraid that, if the Esperantists themselves did not now revise the whole language, future governments, after adopting Esperanto, would commission revision, not by Esperantists, but by scientists who would possibly not have the necessary competence. Zamenhof's last words addressed to the whole Esperanto community expressed this view:

We must, then, find a solution to the unhappy question that constantly hangs over our language like the sword of Damocles. We must, once and for all, very attentively and in detail, revise our entire language.

(Zamenhof 1971: 203)

The war turned Zamenhof's life upside down. On November 22, he suffered a heart attack. Following his recovery, he started to share his professional work with his son Adam, who saw patients in the morning, while his father saw them for two hours in the afternoon. From then on, Zamenhof could devote himself to Esperanto in the morning and no longer had to work in the evenings. In March 1915 he completed his translation of the Old Testament and began to translate Andersen's fairy tales (from German).

The Zamenhofs moved from their home in Dzika Street in July 1915 and took up residence in a street with a more suitable name: Królewska (Royal Street). The rest of Zamenhof's life was spent in this comfortable, seven-room apartment on the third floor of the attractive house at number 141, in the best district in Warsaw, close to the central city park. His son Adam took over his practice in Dzika Street. Zamenhof did not agree to stop working entirely, but he was allowed only very few patients.

A few days after the Zamenhofs' move, the Russian army withdrew from Warsaw and the city was occupied by the Germans. The atmosphere of war continually saddened Zamenhof, who had devoted his life to the peaceful reunification of humanity. Many Esperantists were dying on the battlefields. Particularly upsetting for Zamenhof was the death on July 18, 1916, of his youngest brother, Alexander, the most ardent Zionist in the family. He worried about his daughter Sophia, who had begun working for her uncle, Constantine Zilbernik, in the Kharkov administrative district and, after the Russian army's withdrawal, was unable to return to Warsaw, now under German occupation.

Esperantist activity withered during the war. Esperantists visited Królewska Street only on rare occasions. Among the visitors were Leo Belmont, Odo Bujwid, Edward Wiesenfeld and the German Esperantist Major Paul Neubarth, the port commandant in Warsaw. Beginning in August 1916, Antoni Grabowski regularly visited Zamenhof to read fragments of his translation of Adam Mickiewicz's *Pan Tadeusz*.

Zamenhof never stopped working on his *Homaranism* project and, two months before his death, he sent the final version to the German lawyer Ludwig Schiff. He asked Schiff to translate it into German and send it on to de Saussure so that the latter could add the French translation, have the text printed, and distribute it to the world's most important periodicals.

Like the previous ones, this version consisted of a foreword and a declaration. The foreword distinguished clearly between Esperantism and *Homaranism* and outlined a completely new definition of the doctrine:

> Under the name "*Homaranism*" I mean a striving towards "a brotherhood of humanity", towards the eradication of interracial hatred and injustice and towards a way of life that, little by little, could lead, not in theory, but in practice, to a spiritual union of all human beings.
>
> (*Homaranism*, 1917: *Mi estas Homo* 235)

It is noteworthy that Zamenhof no longer envisions the idea that "humans will some day merge into a single neutrally human people", as he did in the first version of *homaranism*. Now it is a question of striving towards "a spiritual union of all human beings".

An analysis of the four versions of this philosophy (*Hillelism*, 1906; *Homaranism*, 1906; *Homaranism*, 1913; *Homaranism*, 1917) reveals that Zamenhof attributed less and less importance to the problem of language. Esperanto is not mentioned at all in 1913 and 1917, and the 1917 version even omits all mention of the neutrally human language. Zamenhof's target audience had changed. The first universal project (Hillelism, 1906) took into account the interests of the Russian Jews, but this consideration later disappeared. The final version of *Homaranism* was intended by Zamenhof to be disseminated, not in the Esperanto community, but in the entire world, and not through Esperanto, but through the major national languages.

Indeed, striving to bring about a brotherhood of humanity, the eradication of interracial hatred and a spiritual union of all human beings is a more general goal than that of achieving linguistic and religious unity. Furthermore, the guiding principle of *Homaranism* ("Do unto others as you would have them do unto you" in the final version) is not religious, but moral. The concept of striving towards a brotherhood of humanity and the application of the above-mentioned principle (also of "tolerance," which is implicit in *Homaranism* although not explicitly named) could make *Homaranism* attractive, less to Esperantists and religious believers than to ordinary "progressives," for whom language and religious problems were not of utmost importance.

A few weeks before his death, Zamenhof began writing his last essay, *On God and Eternal Life*, which he considered very important, even though he expected that his sudden expression of religious belief would be subject to much criticism. Unfortunately, after the introduction there is nothing but a one-paragraph description of his loss of religious belief during his early childhood. Besides this paragraph, all that remains of the projected article is a small sheet of paper with an outline of the content and two sentences written in the right-hand margin: "I began to feel that perhaps death is not a disappearance, but a miracle, and that there exist some kind of laws in nature by which something guides us to some kind of destination..." and "everyone probably has some vaguely felt belief, for otherwise their life would have no more meaning than that of an animal" (*On God and Eternal Life*, 1917: *Mi estas Homo* 245).

This was his last, unfinished, ideological writing. In it, Zamenhof says he "reflected a great deal and read various scientific and philosophical works," but it is not known which specific works he meant. His own writings, especially the earliest ones, were influenced by the ideas of the already fading Haskala movement, by Pinsker's autoemancipation, Dubnov's autonomism, Herzl's political Zionism, and especially the spiritual Zionism of Ahad Ha'am.

Zamenhof's ideas were, to different degrees, related to the ideals of the French Revolution, the American "melting pot", Russian cosmism, cosmopolitanism, Christian ecumenism, freemasonry, the Bahai faith, and so on. The influences of the Russian philosopher and poet Vladimir Solovyov, the German Jewish philosopher Hermann Cohen, and the French philosopher Auguste Comte are evident in his works.

He was unable to finish his last essay, because his weakness made it too difficult for him to write. On the afternoon of the April 14, 1917, in German-occupied Warsaw, Ludovic Lazarus Zamenhof's heart stopped beating.

Zamenhof was dead, but he left behind his children (they were all murdered by the Nazis during the Second World War), his Esperanto language, which was his gift to the world, his translations, and his ideas, which even today still inspire those who consider themselves, not just members of an ethnic group or a religion but members of the human race, members of the brotherhood of humanity, who believe in its unity in diversity.

UPDATE ON ESPERANTO

Teaching and learning Esperanto:

Communicative ability in Esperanto can be rapidly acquired, so it is an ideal introduction to foreign-language study. Within weeks, students can begin to use Esperanto for correspondence, and within months for school trips abroad. Positive effects of prior learning of Esperanto on the study of both first and second languages are widely documented (see *www.springboard2languages.org/home.htm*, on current work in the U.K.). Despite its potential contribution to the language curriculum, however, Esperanto is rarely included in national education or language policies (one present exception is Hungary, where it can be studied as part of the national language examination system). Most people learn it through the internet (*www.lernu.net*), self-study, correspondence (particularly e-mail), or local Esperanto clubs. Textbooks and self-instruction materials for Esperanto exist in over 100 languages: see *www. edukado.net*.

Works Cited

Esperantisto. 1894, Number 1.

Esperantisto. 1895, Number 3.

Kohen-Cedek, J. 1969. L. L. Zamenhof kaj la aramea lingvo (L. L. Zamenhof and the Aramaic Language). Adolf Holzhaus, ed. *Doktoro kaj lingvo Esperanto.* Helsinki: Fondumo Esperanto.

Lins, Ulrich. 1988. *La danĝera lingvo: Studo pri la persekutoj kontraŭ Esperanto.* Gerlingen:Bleicher.

Ludovikito [Itô Kanzi], ed. 1987. *Ludovikologiaj biografietoj.* Kyoto: Ludovikito (*Iam kompletigota plena verkaro de L. L. Zamenhof;* Supplementary volume 3).

Maimon, N.Z. 1978. *La kaŝita vivo de Zamenhof.* Tokyo: Japana Esperanto-Instituto.

[Zamenhof, L.] D-ro Esperanto. 1888. *Aldono al la Dua Libro de l'Lingvo Internacia.* Warsaw, 1888.

Zamenhof, L. 1992. *Fundamenta krestomatio de la lingvo Esperanto.* 18th edn., ed. Gaston Waringhien. Rotterdam: Universala Esperanto-Asocio.

Zamenhof, L.L. 1911. International language. G. Spiller, ed. *Papers on Inter-Racial Problems Communicated to the First Universal Races Congress.* London: P. S. King & Son.

Zamenhof, L.L. 1971. Historia manuskripto de Zamenhof. *Esperanto* 64/12:202-203.

Waringhien, Gaston, ed. 1948. *Leteroj de L.-L. Zamenhof. La tragedio de lia vivo rivelita en lia ĵus retrovita korespondo kun la francaj eminentuloj.* 2 volumes. Paris: SAT.

Ludovikito [Itô Kanzi], ed. 1989–1991. Iom reviziita plena verkaro de L. L. Zamenhof. 3 volumes. Kyoto: Ludovikito.

Korĵenkov, Aleksander, ed. 2006. *Mi estas homo.* Kaliningrad: Sezonoj / Kaunas: Litova Esperanto-Asocio.

All known works of Zamenhof (including translations and textbooks) are contained in the 58-volume collected works edited by Itô Kanzi under the pseudonym Ludovikito (*Plena Verkaro de L.L. Zamenhof*), but the bulk of this material consists of related literary, historical and scholarly texts.

A brief bibliography of works on Zamenhof

Privat's *Life* (1931) is now somewhat dated. If we except the present work, still the only authoritative comprehensive biography in English is Boulton (1960), though a new study is in preparation by Esther Schor, and a German-language biography is in progress by Andreas Künzli. Centassi & Masson (1995) provide a biography in French. Dobrzynski's (2003) popularised retelling of the memoirs of Zamenhof's grandson Louis Zaleski-Zamenhof is available in many languages, though not yet in English. Minnaja (2009) offers an Italian-language anthology of Zamenhof's writings, and Heller a biography of Zamenhof's younger daughter.

Banet-Fornalowa, Zofia. 2000. *La familio Zamenhof*. La Chaux-de-Fonds, Switzerland: Kooperativo de Literatura Foiro.

Boulton, Marjorie. 1960. *Zamenhof, Creator of Esperanto*. London: Routledge & Kegan Paul.

Centassi, René & Henri Masson. 1995. *L'Homme qui a défié Babel*. Paris: Éditions Ramsay.

Dobrzynski, Roman. 2003. *La Zamenhof-Strato*. Kaunas: Varpas. [Available in translation in over ten languages, including French, Italian, Portuguese, Polish, Lithuanian, and Slovenian]

Heller, Wendy. 1985. *Lidia, Daughter of Esperanto*. Oxford: George Ronald.

Holzhaus, Adolf. 1969. *Doktoro kaj lingvo Esperanto*. Helsinki: Fondumo Esperanto.

Kiselman, Christer. 2010. Hilelismo, homaranismo kaj neŭtrale-homa religio. Detlev Blanke & Ulrich Lins, eds. *La arto labori kune*. Rotterdam: Universala Esperanto-Asocio. 401-414.

Korĵenkov, Aleksander. 2009. *Homarano: La vivo, verkoj kaj ideoj de d-ro L. L. Zamenhof*. Kaliningrad: Sezonoj / Kaunas: Litova Esperanto-Asocio.

Künzli, Andreas. 2009. Neŭtrala lingvo kaj nova humanisma etiko – la celado de d-ro L. L. Zamenhof. *Esperanto* 102/2:34-35.

Künzli, Andreas. 2009. *Svislando en la vivo de Zamenhof.* Literatura Foiro 40/4:172-183.

Künzli, Andreas. 2009. Inter cionismo kaj reformjudismo. *Spegulo* 2/4:207-225.

Lapenna, Ivo, ed. 1960. *Memorlibro eldonita okaze de la centjara datreveno de la naskiĝo de d-ro L. L. Zamenhof.* London: Universala Esperanto-Asocio – Centro de Esploro kaj Dokumentado.

Lieberman, E. James. 1979. Esperanto and trans-national identity: The case of Dr. Zamenhof. *International Journal of the Sociology of Language* 20:89-108.

Lins, Ulrich. 2007. Esperanto oder das Dilemma des Dr. Zamenhof. Gisela Dachs, ed. *Sprachen. Jüdischer Almanach des Leo Baeck Instituts.* Frankfurt am Main: Jüdischer Verlag im Suhrkamp Verlag. 127-140.

Maimon, N. Z. 1978. *La kaŝita vivo de Zamenhof.* Tokyo: Japana Esperanto-Instituto.

Minnaja, Carlo, ed. 2009. *Lazzaro Ludovico Zamenhof: Antologia.* Milano: Federazione Esperantista Italiana.

Minnaja, Carlo. 2009. Fajron sentis li interne. *Literatura Foiro* 40/1:7-13.

Ošlak, Vinko. 2009. Zamenhof kaj lia etiko. *Literatura Foiro* 40/5:230-239.

Privat, Edmond. 2007. *Vivo de Zamenhof.* 6th edition, ed. Ulrich Lins. Rotterdam: Universala Esperanto-Asocio.

Privat, Edmond. 1931. *The Life of Zamenhof,* trans. Ralph Eliott. London: Allen & Unwin.

Romaniuk, Zbigniew & Tomasz Wiśniewski. 2009. *Ĉio komenciĝis ĉe la Verda. Pri Ludoviko Zamenhof, lia familio kaj la komenco de Esperanto / Zaczęło się na Zielonej. O Ludowiku Zamenhofie, jego rodzinie i początkach esperanta.* Łódź: KSIĘŻ MŁYN.

Shemer, Josef. 2009. 'Mi estas judo.' *Esperanto* 102/3:57-58.

Waringhien, Gaston. 1980. *1887 kaj la sekvo.* Antwerp/La Laguna: TK/Stafeto.

A brief bibliography of works on Esperanto

Esperanto and the Esperanto movement

Janton (1993), Mullarney (1989), Richardson (1988), and Tonkin's encyclopedia entry (2009) offer useful introductions in English. Reagan (2005, 2009) addresses criticisms of Esperanto. Forster (1982) provides a sociological study of the British Esperanto movement, and Lins (1986) looks at the work of the Universal Esperanto Association.

Auld, William. 1988. *La fenomeno Esperanto*. Rotterdam: Universala Esperanto-Asocio

Blanke, Detlev. 2009. Causes of the relative success of Esperanto. *Language Problems & Language Planning* 33/3:251-266.

Carlton, Edward. 1990. *Towards a Better Understanding: Esperanto, the Universal Secondary and Intermediary Language*. East Wittering, England: Gooday.

Forster, Peter G. 1982. *The Esperanto Movement*. The Hague: Mouton.

Janton, Pierre. 1993. *Esperanto: Language, Literature, and Community*, ed. Humphrey Tonkin, trans. Humphrey Tonkin, Jane Edwards, Karen Johnson-Weiner. Albany, NY: State University of New York Press.

Janton, Pierre. 1977. *L'espéranto*. 2nd edn. Paris: Presses Universitaires de France.

Kökény, Lajos & Vilmos Bleier. 1933. *Enciklopedio de Esperanto*. 2 vols. Budapest: Literatura Mondo. (Rpt. in one volume, Budapest: Hungara Esperanto-Asocio, 1979.)

Lapenna, Ivo, Ulrich Lins & Tazio Carlevaro. 1974. *Esperanto en perspektivo: Faktoj kaj analizoj pri la Internacia Lingvo*. London & Rotterdam: Centro de Esploro kaj Dokumentado pri la Monda Lingvo-Problemo.

Lins, Ulrich. 1986. *The Contribution of the Universal Esperanto Association to World Peace*. Esperanto Documents 37A. Rotterdam: Universala Esperanto-Asocio

Mullarney, Maire. 1989. *Esperanto for Hope: A New Way of Learning the Language of Peace.* Dublin: Poolberg.

Reagan, Timothy. 2009. *Language Matters: Reflections on Educational Linguistics.* Charlotte, NC: Information Age Publishing.

Reagan, Timothy. 2005. *Critical Questions, Critical Perspectives: Language and the Second Language Educator.* Greenwich, CT: Information Age Publishing.

Richardson, David. 1988. *Esperanto: Learning and Using the International Language.* Eastsound WA: Orcas.

Richmond, Ian, ed. 1993. *Aspects of Internationalism: Language and Culture.* Lanham MD: University Press of America.

Tonkin, Humphrey. 2009. *Una lingua e un popolo: Problemi attuali del movimento esperantista,* ed. Carlo Minnaja, trans. Elvia Belluco. Venafro: Edizioni Eva.

Tonkin, Humphrey. 2009. Esperanto. Akira Iriye & Pierre-Yves Saunier, ed. *The Palgrave Dictionary of Transnational History.* Basingstoke & New York: Palgrave Macmillan. 344-345

Tonkin, Humphrey, ed. 1997. *Esperanto, Interlinguistics, and Planned Language.* Lanham MD: University Press of America.

The language

Gledhill (1998) and Wennergren (2005) provide comprehensive grammatical studies; Wells (1978) provides a readable introduction. The scholarly literature is surveyed by Blanke (2003) and Tonkin (1993, 2007). The major Esperanto-Esperanto dictionary is Duc Goninaz (2002); the best English two-way dictionary is Wells (2010). Maxwell (1988) reviews work on second-language acquisition of Esperanto.

Blanke, Detlev. 2003. Interlinguistics and Esperanto studies: Paths to the scholarly literature. *Language Problems & Language Planning* 27/2:155-192.

Duc Goninaz, Michel, and others. 2002. *La nova plena ilustrita vortaro de Esperanto*. Paris: SAT.

Duc Goninaz, Michel. 1974. Les influences slaves en espéranto. *Cahiers de linguistique, d'orientalisme et de slavistique* (Université de Provence) 3-4:31-53.

Duličenko, Aleksandr. 1988. Esperanto: A unique model for general linguistics. *Language Problems & Language Planning* 12:148-151.

Fiedler, Sabine. 1999. *Plansprache und Phraseologie: Empirische Untersuchungen zu reproduziertem Sprachmaterial im Esperanto*. Frankfurt/Main: Peter Lang.

Gledhill, Christopher. 1998. *The Grammar of Esperanto: A Corpus-based Description*. München / Newcastle. LINCOM Europa.

Maxwell, Dan. 1988. On the acquisition of Esperanto. *Studies in Second Language Acquisition*. 10:51-61.

Schubert, Klaus 1992. Esperanto as an intermediate language for machine translation. John Newton, ed. *Computers in Translation. A Practical Appraisal*. London & New York: Routledge. 78-95.

Schubert, Klaus. 1988. Ausdruckskraft und Regelmässigkeit: Was Esperanto für automatische Übersetzung geeignet macht. *Language Problems & Language Planning* 12:130-147.

Symoens, Edward. 1995. *Bibliografio de disertacioj pri Esperanto kaj interlingvistiko*. Rotterdam: Universala Esperanto-Asocio.

Tonkin, Humphrey. 2007. Recent studies in Esperanto and interlinguistics: 2006. *Language Problems & Language Planning* 31/2:169-196.

Tonkin, Humphrey. 1993. Esperanto studies: An overview. Ian M. Richmond, ed. *Aspects of Internationalism: Language and Culture*. 9–20.

Versteegh, Kees. 1993. Esperanto as first language: Acquisition with a restricted input. *Linguistics* 31:539-555.

Wells, John Christopher. 2010. *English-Esperanto-English Dictionary*. New York: Mondial.

Wells, John C. 1978. *Lingvistikaj aspektoj de Esperanto*. Rotterdam: Universala Esperanto-Asocio.

Wennergren, Bertilo. 2005. *Plena manlibro de Esperanta gramatiko*. El Cerrito CA: Esperanto League for North America.

The literature

Sutton (2008) provides a detailed English-language overview. Auld (1984) offers a comprehensive anthology of Esperanto poetry. Tonkin (1993, 2002) can serve as introductions for the English-language reader.

Auld, William, ed. 1984. *Esperanta antologio 1887-1981*. Rotterdam: Universala Esperanto-Asocio

Gregor, Douglas B. 1979. *The Cultural Value of Esperanto*. Esperanto Documents 19A. Rotterdam: Universal Esperanto Association. [Originally published in an earlier version in the journal *Modern Languages*, 1965.]

Pleadin, Josip, ed. 2006. *Ordeno de verda plumo: Leksikono pri Esperantlingvaj verkistoj*. Durdevac, Croatia: Grafokom.

Sutton, Geoffrey. 2008. *Concise Encyclopedia of the Original Literature of Esperanto*. New York: Mondial

Tonkin, Humphrey. 1993. Esperanto poetry. Alex Preminger & T. V. F. Brogan, ed. *The New Princeton Encyclopedia of Poetry and Poetics*. Princeton: Princeton University Press. 381-382.

Tonkin, Humphrey. 2002. The role of literary language in Esperanto. Klaus Schubert, ed. *Planned Languages: From Concept to Reality.* Brussels: Hogeschool voor Wetenschap en Kunst. 11-35.

The history of Esperanto

There is no comprehensive English-language history of Esperanto. Minnaja (2007) provides an Italian-language history of the movement in that country. Sikosek offers a German-language history of the Universal Esperanto Association (2006), and Lins (1988) a German-language history of persecutions of Esperantists, especially in Nazi Germany and Stalinist USSR.

Hou Zhiping. 2004. *Konciza historio de la ĉina Esperanto-movado.* Beijing: Nova Stelo.

Korĵenkov, Aleksander. 2005. *Historio de Esperanto.* Kaliningrad: Sezonoj.

Lins, Ulrich. 1988. *Die gefährliche Sprache.* Gerlingen: Bleicher.

Lins, Ulrich. 2008. Esperanto as language and idea in China and Japan. *Language Problems & Language Planning* 32/1:47-60.

Ludovikito [Itô Kanzi]. 1998. *Historieto de Esperanto.* Tokio: Libroteko Tokio.

Minnaja, Carlo. 2007. *L'Esperanto in Italia: alla ricerca della democrazia linguistica.* Padova: Poligrafo.

Müller-Saini, Gotelind & Gregor Benton. 2006. Esperanto and Chinese anarchism 1907-1920: The translation from diaspora to homeland. *Language Problems & Language Planning* 30/1:45-73.

Müller-Saini, Gotelind & Gregor Benton. 2006. Esperanto and Chinese anarchism in the 1920s and 1930s. *Language Problems & Language Planning* 30/2:173-192.

Poblet i Feijoo, Francesc. 2004. *Els inicis del moviment esperantista a Catalunya / La komenca esperanto-movado en Katalunio.* Tarragona: O Limaco Edizions.

Privat, Edmond. 1927. *Historio de la lingvo Esperanto: la movado 1900-1927.* Leipzig: Ferdinand Hirt.

Sikosek, Ziko Marcus. 2005. *Sed homoj kun homoj.* Rotterdam: Universala Esperanto-Asocio.

Sikosek, Marcus. 2004. Books and their association. *Language Problems & Language Planning* 28/1:25-44.

Sikosek, Marcus. 2006. *Die neutrale Sprache: Eine politische Geschichte des Esperanto-Weltbundes.* Bydgoszcz, Poland: Skonpres.

van Dijk, Ziko. 2008. *La Asocio: Skizoj kaj studoj pri la historio de Universala Esperanto-Asocio.* Antverpeno: Flandra Esperanto-Ligo.

The application of Esperanto

Harry and Mandel (1979) present the famous Harry Plan for the introduction of Esperanto at the United Nations. Lapenna's three studies examine the situation of Esperanto at the League of Nations and the UN. Piron (1994) presents arguments for the use of Esperanto and rebuts arguments against it. Fettes (2003) and Pool & Fettes (1998) explore alternative approaches to interlingual communication.

Fettes, Mark. 2003. The geostrategies of interlingualism. Jacques Maurais & Michael A. Morris, ed. *Languages in a globalising world.* Cambridge: Cambridge University Press. 37-46.

Harry, Ralph L. & Mark Mandel. 1979. *Language Equality in International Cooperation.* Esperanto Documents 21A. Rotterdam: Universal Esperanto Association.

Lapenna, Ivo. 1969. La situation juridique des langues sous le régime des Nations Unies. *La Monda Lingvo-Problemo* 1:87-106.

Lapenna, Ivo. 1969. La situation juridique des "langues officielles" avant la fondation des Nations Unies. *La Monda Lingvo-Problemo* 1:5-18.

Lapenna, Ivo. 1970-71. The common language question before international organizations. *La Monda Lingvo-Problemo* 2:83-102, 3:11-30.

Piron, Claude. 1994. *Le Défi des langues. Du gâchis au bon sens.* Paris: L'Harmattan.

Pool, Jonathan & Mark Fettes. 1998. The challenge of interlingualism: A research invitation. *Esperantic Studies* 10:1-3.

Tonkin, Humphrey. 1982. *Esperanto in the Service of the United Nations.* Esperanto Documents 27A. Rotterdam: Universala Esperanto-Asocio.

Tonkin, H. 1996. Language hierarchy at the United Nations. Sylvie Léger, ed. *Vers un agenda linguistique: Regard futuriste sur les Nations Unies / Towards a Language Agenda: Futurist Outlook on the United Nations.* Ottawa: Canadian Centre for Linguistic Rights, U of Ottawa. 3-28.

Planned languages

Eco (1995) looks at the history of language invention, and Okrent (2009) at the current scene. Blanke (1985) offers an authoritative German-language overview. Schubert (1989) and Schubert & Maxwell (2002) provide a scholarly approach. Künzli's multilingual encyclopedia (2006) addresses the role of Switzerland.

Blanke, Detlev. 1985. *Internationale Plansprachen: Eine Einführung.* Berlin: Akademie-Verlag.

Blanke, Detlev. 2006. *Interlinguistische Beiträge. Studien zum Wesen und zur Funktion internationaler Plansprachen*, ed. Sabine Fiedler. Frankfurt/Main: Peter Lang.

Conley, Tim & Stephen Cain. 2006. *Encyclopedia of Fictional and Fantastic Languages*. Westport CT & London: Greenwood.

Couturat, Louis & Léopold Leau. 1903+1907/2001. *Histoire de la langue universelle 1903. Les nouvelles langues internationales 1907. Mit einem bibliographischen Nachwort von Reinhard Haupenthal*. Hildesheim, Zürich & New York: Olms.

Eco, Umberto. 1995. *The Search for the Perfect Language*, trans. James Fentress. Oxford & Cambridge MA: Blackwell.

Künzli, Andreas. 2006. *Universalaj lingvoj en Svislando*. La Chaux-de-Fonds, Switzerland: SES & CDELI.

Large, Andrew. 1985. *The Artificial Language Movement*. Oxford: Blackwell.

Okrent, Arika. 2009. *In the Land of Invented Languages*. New York: Spiegel & Grau.

Schubert, Klaus, ed. 2002. *Planned Languages: From Concept to Reality*. Brussels: Hogeschool voor Wetenschap en Kunst.

Schubert, Klaus, & Dan Maxwell, ed. 1989. *Interlinguistics: Aspects of the Science of Planned Languages*. Berlin, New York, Amsterdam: Mouton de Gruyter.

Notes

1 As a citizen of Russia, Zamenhof was formally named Lazar' Markovitch Zamenhof. This particular form, consisting of the personal name, the father's personal name and the family name, in that order, was obligatory in Russia. To avoid confusion, he will be referred to in this text by the name he adopted later and by which he is generally known: Ludovic Lazarus Zamenhof or L. L. Zamenhof, as he usually signed himself.

2 Formed in 1569, the Polish-Lithuanian Commonwealth extended from the Baltic almost as far as the Black Sea and included not only modern Lithuania and Poland, but also Belarus and Ukraine. The Commonwealth broke apart in 1795.

3 Hasidism is a spiritual movement that arose among Eastern European Jews in the 1700s. It teaches that one can become closer to God through emotion and devotion to the Torah rather than through the intellect.

4 75% of the working population of Russian Jews were tradespeople or merchants in the mid-nineteenth century.

5 The Maskilim were adherents of the Jewish Haskalah movement, which had begun in Germany during the Age of Enlightenment and was heavily influenced by the ideas of the Enlightenment philosophers.

6 The Real School was a secondary school that put more emphasis than the Gymnasium on practical subjects.

7 The first Volapük textbook was published in the spring of 1880 by the pastor Johann Martin Schleyer from Baden. The language spread quickly, clubs and journals were established in a number of countries, and international Volapük conventions were held in 1884, 1887 and 1889. However, its popularity rapidly waned in the 1890s, in part because of the advent of Esperanto.

8 Idiom Neutral, published in 1902, began as a much modified version of Volapük, but by the time of its publication was a distinctly new language. Its name means "Neutral Language".

9 The Tolstoyans were adherents of the philosophical ideas of the great Russian novelist Tolstoy. Essentially, they studied the teachings of Jesus Christ and recognized no authority but that of God. Their refusal to recognize secular authority made them suspect in the eyes of the Russian government. The Posrednik publishing company was launched in 1884 to publish works accessible to the Russian peasants, to act as the "intermediary" between Russian culture and literature and the peasant class.

10 The Esperanto flag is green with a white star. Green is also the colour of the star Esperantists often wear on their lapel to identify themselves as Esperanto speakers.

11 The correlative words in Esperanto are a logically defined set of words that express the ideas of "that, what/which, some, every, no". Their structure is logical: *kiu* = who, what, which; *iu* = someone; *kie* = where; *ie* = somewhere; *nenie* = nowhere; etc.

12 Monosemy means that each word has only one meaning.

13 The concept of reversibility is based on the assumption that, because the words of the language are formed from invariable elements (for example, Esperanto's affixes), it is possible to derive from any given word all other words of the same semantic group. Thus, from the word "vendisto" (salesperson) it is possible to derive the infinitive "vendi" (to sell), the noun "vendejo" (shop, store), the adjective "vendebla" (saleable), etc. From any one of these words, it is possible to derive all the others.

14 There was a general dissatisfaction with the rule of the Czars that led to strikes and a revolt in Russia during this period, especially following the massacre of about 1,000 demonstrators at the Czar's Winter Palace in January 1905. This period set the stage for the later Bolshevik revolution of 1917 that ended the rule of the Czars and ushered in the period of communist rule.

15 Nahum Sokolow was a leading Zionist at the time. He was a journalist and a prolific Hebrew author.

16 The links between *Homaranismo* and Esperantism did not go unnoticed in the world, however. On June 8, 1940, for example, a report by the State Office for Security summed up the Nazis' relationship to Esperanto as follows:

> The Polish Jew Zamenhof, an eye doctor in Warsaw in his day, came out of the Zionist movement (Chovevey Zion). He strove to bring about the Jewish reign over the world, as prophesied in Isaiah 2:2-4, the reign of peace under Jewish rule. All races were to voluntarily subjugate themselves to the Jews. This goal was to be achieved by "peaceful" penetration and decomposition of the master races. The tools used by Zamenhof were unbridled pacifism, a new religion, *homaranismo*, initiated by him as a preparatory step towards the Jewish religion, and the universal language invented by him, "Esperanto", which, through the same reading material for people of all races, colours and geographical origins, through the same education, ideals, beliefs and goals was to lead gradually to a general racial stew.
>
> These three goals together, not just the promotion of a universal language, make up Esperantism, which, after about 1905, has served as an auxiliary weapon of the Jews.
>
> [...]
>
> To consider "Esperanto" as just an auxiliary language for international communication is wrong. The artificial language Esperanto is part of Esperantism, of the weapon of the Jews.
>
> (Lins 124, 127)

LaVergne, TN USA
19 December 2010
209390LV00003B/90/P